WHY WE
SPEND TOO
MUCH ON
HEALTH CARE

WHY WE SPEND TOO MUCH ON HEALTH CARE

AND WHAT WE CAN DO ABOUT IT

By Joseph L. Bast,
Richard C. Rue, and
Stuart A. Wesbury, Jr.

THE HEARTLAND INSTITUTE

■ Chicago ■ Cleveland ■ Detroit ■ Kansas City
■ Milwaukee ■ St. Louis

Printed in the United States of America
British Cataloging in Publication Information Available

Distributed by arrangement with
National Book Network
4720 Boston Way
Lanham, Maryland 20706

3 Henrietta Street
London WC2E 8LU England

Library of Congress Cataloging-in-Publication Data

Bast, Joseph L.
Why we spend too much on health care : and what we can do about it
/ by Joseph L. Bast, Richard C. Rue, and Stuart A. Wesbury, Jr. —
2nd ed.
p.   cm.
Includes index.
1. Medical care, Cost of—United States.   2. Medical policy—
United States.   I. Rue, Richard.   II. Wesbury, Stuart A.   III. Title.
RA410.53.B38   1993
338.4'33621'0973—dc20   93–9710 CIP

ISBN 0–9632027–2–3 (pbk. : alk. paper)

 The paper used in this publication meets the minimum requirements of
American National Standard for Information Sciences—Permanence
of Paper for Printed Library Materials, ANSI Z39.48–1984.

Contents

Acknowledgements

We wish to thank the following people who reviewed early drafts of the manuscript and provided many useful comments. Any remaining errors are solely the responsibility of the authors.

Dean Baim
Ralph O. Butz, M.D.
Franklin M. Buchta
Joe E. Bell
John Burke
Rod Casavant
Douglas Cocks
John Conant
Alain Enthoven
Bradley J. Furnish
Robert J. Genetski
Jesse S. Hixson
Harold Hotelling
Richard H. Keehn
David L. Littmann

Conrad Meier
Arthur A. Nolan, Jr.
John North
David Olson
David Osterfeld
David H. Padden
William S. Peirce
Frank Resnik
J. Patrick Rooney
Lee Tooman
Thomas Ulen
Tom Walton
Tom Wyrick
Philip Zazove, M.D.

We also thank the many donors to The Heartland Institute whose financial support made this book possible. Special thanks to The Daniel F. and Ada L. Rice Foundation, Golden Rule Insurance Company, Eli Lilly and Co., and Time Insurance Co. for their generous help.

John Goodman, president of the National Center for Policy Analysis (NCPA), was the inspiration for many of the book's better thoughts. Samuel Brunelli, president of the American Legislative Exchange Council (ALEC), and his excellent staff were also very helpful.

Foreword

HEALTH CARE REFORM is one of the most urgent needs facing America today. The high and rising cost of health care threatens to bankrupt individuals and small businesses, while millions of Americans no longer can afford to buy health insurance. Serious charges are being leveled against the quality of America's health care system, and proposals for reform that can only be called *radical* are seriously discussed in Washington D.C. and in state capitals around the country.

This environment makes release of the second edition of *Why We Spend Too Much on Health Care* particularly timely. This book provides an excellent overview of the many factors that contribute to high health care costs and unnecessarily high spending levels—two separate issues, as the authors very correctly point out. I strongly recommended the book to my colleagues in Congress when the first edition was released in early 1992, and I am happy now to recommend this revised edition to every concerned American.

With all the charges and counter-charges filling the air, it is sometimes easy to forget that health care in the U.S. is widely and correctly perceived as being the best in the world. U.S. hospitals have the latest in high-tech equipment, are staffed by the world's best-trained specialists, and have the highest success rates for most types of surgical procedures. Medical technology is one of our country's major exports, and thousands of people from countries around the world come to America every year to be treated in our hospitals. This "second to none" system is the envy of the world.

Unfortunately, our national health statistics—infant mortality rates and longevity, in particular—compare unfavorably to those of other nations with inferior health care systems. The reason for this is well-known to professional researchers: the effects of even a magnificent health care system are overshadowed by such factors as lifestyle (especially smoking, drinking, and physical fitness), violent crime and accident rates, teenage pregnancy rates, and other things over which a health care system has little control. Regrettably, proponents of "nationalizing" America's health care system have shamelessly used infant mortality rates and longevity to claim that health care systems in other countries are better than the American system of health care.

The authors of *Why We Spend Too Much on Health Care* expose the faulty reasoning behind this attack on American health care, and they present a more balanced account of how public health and health care delivery in the U.S. compare to those of other countries. This part of the book should be required reading for anyone advocating a "Canadian model" or "German model" for the U.S.

While America's health care system deserves praise for doing some things right, it is wrong to claim that the system is not facing a serious challenge. The data support the contention that spending on health care in the United States is out of control, consuming a record percentage of the nation's wealth and continuing to rise more than 10 percent per year. A growing number of individuals simply cannot afford to purchase health insurance at today's high prices, and consequently their access to health care may be limited. The financial burden on businesses that provide health insurance benefits is reaching crippling levels; small businesses, in particular, are often unable to continue to provide insurance coverage for their employees.

Some people use the rising price of health care as a stick to beat one or more of the industries that make up the health care marketplace. Some say the source of the problem is doctors who gouge their patients and insurance companies. Others blame insurance companies who refuse to cover people with pre-existing conditions. Still others blame lawyers, drug companies, hospital administrators, government regulators, and even consumers themselves. Who is right?

Possibly the most important message contained in *Why We Spend Too Much on Health Care* is this: No one industry or profession bears the blame for high and rising health care spending. The reasons for high spending are simply too numerous to all be traced back to doctors, insurers, or drug companies. And of great importance: Many of the reasons for high spending are legitimate, based on a growing need for health care spending, new medical discoveries, and a willingness by many people to make greater investments in their physical comfort and longevity.

If there are no "bad guys" responsible for the crisis of rising health care costs, why do we spend too much? The authors tick off several reasons: massive government spending on health care, often on a "cost-plus" basis, that bids up prices for other health care consumers; favorable tax treatment of health insurance premiums that encourages employees to trade higher compensation for inflationary "first-dollar" coverage insurance policies; and government regulations such as Medicare regulations, insurance mandates, price controls, and supply restrictions. The authors then present a reform agenda that tackles these root causes of the spending problem.

The essence of effective health care reform requires empowering health consumers, not handing over a vital high-tech industry to government bureaucrats. The authors of this book make a convincing case that national health insurance or its first step, "play or pay," would be a disaster for all Americans. This would be a terrible and perhaps irreversible step in the wrong direction for America, and a step that every informed American should vigorously oppose.

We *can* control spending while maintaining the best quality health care system in the world. We can do this by giving people incentives to shop around, think twice before seeking multiple tests and discretionary medical attention, and weigh the costs and benefits of additional tests and drugs. We can remove costly regulations and mandates that raise prices and lower quality, and we can change a tax policy that distorts incentives and fuels the upward spiral of health care spending. By allowing the normal market processes to work in the health care marketplace, we can force out expensive and inefficient producers who now are free to gouge patients and their insurers.

The issues addressed in this book have never been more

important or more timely than today. Every American owes it to
himself or herself to become informed about the national debate
over health care reform. This book is an excellent place to start.

— Hon. Richard Armey
Congressman, Texas

Introduction

THE HIGH COST of health care in the U.S. is the key issue in the national debate over reforming the nation's health care system. Surveys show that the high cost of employee health care is among business' highest concerns.[1] The promise of lower costs figured prominently in the American College of Physicians' call in 1990 for a publicly funded "comprehensive and coordinated program to assure access [to health care] on a nationwide basis."[2] Critics of U.S. health care routinely focus on the system's cost and point to European systems, where spending is much less.[3]

Advocates of national health insurance and its twin, socialized medicine, have used the issue of health care costs to build a coalition for their cause. They promise substantial cost savings by adopting a "universal-access single-payer system." One report even claims that the money saved by nationalizing the health insurance industry would be enough to extend health insurance to the entire population of uninsureds.[4] Organized labor, the elderly, and even some parts of the business community have accepted this rhetoric and climbed on board the nationalization bandwagon.

Why should the advocates of nationalization be believed when they place blame for high costs on the health care industry, rather than on the many other factors that affect the cost of health care? At a time when "privatization" is taking place around the world and across the U.S., why should we believe that a centrally planned and tax-financed system will operate more efficiently than a private health care system?

This book takes aim at the health care spending issue. We ask *why* costs are high and how we know that spending is "too high." We challenge the notion that countries with nationalized health care systems have controlled the cost of health care. And we suggest a reform agenda that addresses the real causes of unnecessarily high spending.

Although this book focuses on spending, it also addresses the related issues of access to care and cost shifting. These important matters would be resolved more easily if the problem of rising health costs were addressed successfully. Most of the discussion of these topics occurs in Chapters 4 and 5, and the solutions presented in Chapter 6 specifically address access and cost shifting.

In Chapter 1, meaning is sought for the phrase "too much" in the context of health care spending. How can spending levels in other sectors of the U.S. economy, in the past, or in other nations be relevant when the factors that must be "held constant" are so numerous and influential? Are estimates of health care spending and Gross Domestic Product (GDP) sufficiently accurate or comparable to allow for meaningful analysis? And what does it mean to say that spending on health care is "too high" when the benefits of spending are subjective—relief from pain, return to work, extended life—and therefore known only to individuals?

In Chapter 2 we set aside our objections to the validity of international comparisons and examine what data *are* available. Spending levels in the U.S. appear very high compared to levels in other nations, a finding already widely reported. But surprisingly, spending *trends* in the U.S. hardly distinguish it from other countries during the past 30 years. For example, Japan, Italy, France, and West Germany increased per-capita spending faster than did the U.S. since 1960, and Canada and Australia came within a few percentage points of the U.S. performance.

We then ask *why* health care spending in the U.S. is high. Too often in debates over health care policy it is assumed that high spending levels are necessarily bad. But what if there are legitimate reasons for high levels of spending on health care—reasons that would make the U.S. stand out as a high-spending nation *even if* our systems of delivering and financing health services were the most efficient in the world? Would it still follow that spending on health care is "too high" and should be reduced? The logical answer is no.

In fact, many factors explain why health care is more costly and spending levels higher in the U.S. than in other nations. Chapter 3 documents that wealth, geography, demographics, and public health problems in the U.S. are often without parallel in other countries. The U.S., for example, is geographically huge compared to European countries, its population is extraordinarily diverse, and its social and cultural heritage leads it to choose institutional forms that are much different from those selected in other countries.

The fact that health care spending is neither "out of control" nor entirely unjustified does not mean current levels of spending are acceptable. The market for health care in the U.S. is heavily regulated, profoundly influenced by government spending, and distorted by tax policies that cause over-reliance on health insurance. Chapter 4 describes how this pattern of government intervention has raised spending levels and reduced the efficiency of the U.S. health care system. We find that spending on health care would be substantially lower if government policies were changed, and on this basis we conclude that the U.S. truly does spend "too much" on health care.

Since the cause of overspending lies with government policy, legislation that attempts to assess blame on other parties will not lower health care costs. Unfortunately, such proposals dominate the current debate over health care policy. These proposals include national health insurance, managed competition, mandatory employer-provided insurance ("play or pay") and socialized medicine. In Chapter 5 we survey these proposals and show how, because they have misdiagnosed the cause of the problem, they have no chance of being the cure.

There are better solutions to the problem of rising health care spending. Chapter 6 describes a plan developed by the National Center for Policy Analysis (NCPA) that would lower significantly the cost of health insurance for individuals and employers and allow individuals to pay small medical bills directly from Medical Savings Accounts. The NCPA plan gradually returns health insurance to its original function of insuring against unpredictable major health care needs, and away from its current, inappropriate role as a means for pre-payment of all routine health expenses.

By making individual consumers responsible for more of their health care spending, the NCPA plan touches off a chain of activity in the health care industry that places downward pressure on prices and upward pressure on quality. The difficult problems of access and cross subsidization are substantially, though not completely, addressed by this plan.

Chapter 6 also describes a series of reform proposals put forward by the American Legislative Exchange Council (ALEC) that would lower health care costs while also more directly addressing access issues. The ALEC plan would repeal unnecessary regulation of the health insurance and hospital industries, reform medical liability, and privatize Medicaid through the use of vouchers. This series of reforms aims at the genuine causes of unnecessary health care spending in the U.S., and therefore promises to effect a genuine cure.

The final chapter of the book reminds us of what is at stake in the discussion of health care spending and suggests activities for persons who wish to become part of the national debate. Sources for more information about the NCPA and ALEC plans are presented as well as information about potential allies and resources.

Our findings and proposals are somewhat at odds with conventional wisdom.[5] We believe this is because other researchers have fallen victim to three very attractive, but ultimately deceptive, assumptions: First, that high spending levels *per se* are indicative of a malfunctioning system; second, that standard measures of public health are accurate measures of the outputs of a nation's health care system; and third, that a decentralized and competitive system necessarily is more wasteful and less efficient than a centrally controlled system. Much of this book consists of showing the error of these assumptions.

CHAPTER ONE

What Do We
Mean By "Too Much"?

TOTAL SPENDING on health care in the U.S. was estimated to be $817 billion in 1992.[1] This amount was 14 percent of Gross Domestic Product (GDP), the estimated value of all goods and services produced in the country that year. According to available data, spending on health care is higher in the U.S. than in any other country.

The cost of buying health care affects some of the largest and most influential groups in the country. These groups have become important voices in the public debate over health care policy. They include:

Figure 1-1. *Health Care Spending in the U.S. as a*
Percent of GDP

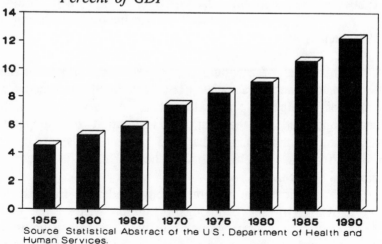

Source Statistical Abstract of the U S. Department of Health and Human Services.

- **Business.** Many employers pay part or all of their employees' health insurance premiums. Those premiums totaled approximately $174 billion in 1990.[2] Recent cost containment efforts by government have resulted in higher insurance premiums for business as hospitals shift costs from Medicaid and Medicare patients to patients with private insurance.[3]

- **Labor.** Health insurance premiums often become part of wage negotiations. In 1989, health benefits were a significant issue in strikes involving more than three-quarters of all striking workers, compared to less than one-fifth in 1986.[4] Organized labor has strongly opposed efforts by business to reduce insurance premiums by raising deductibles, limiting coverage, and increasing copayments.

- **State governments.** State spending for Medicaid reached $34.2 billion in 1990, an increase of 150 percent from 1980.[5] The states are called on increasingly to address the problem of providing health care to persons without health insurance.

- **Families.** Their out-of-pocket spending for health care was estimated to be $162 billion in 1990 alone.[6] The increased reliance on employer-provided health insurance during the 1960s and 1970s meant greater risk of being without insurance during job changes or periods of unemployment during the 1980s and 1990s.

Is this level of spending too high? Most business owners, state legislators, and persons who buy their own insurance or pay directly for medical expenses say it is. A survey of business owners conducted by the National Federation of Independent Business, for example, found that 90.3 percent of the respondents agreed with the statement that "health care is becoming prohibitively expensive."[7]

There is widespread support among academics for this view. Henry J. Aaron of The Brookings Institution writes, "the failure of U.S. efforts to control growth of [health care] spending has been consistent and spectacular."[8] Alain Enthoven and Richard

Kronick of Stanford University contend that "whereas other countries have stabilized the share of their GNP that is spent on health, ours has accelerated in recent years" and "these growing expenditures are adding greatly to deficits in the public sector, threatening the solvency of some industrial companies, and creating heavy burdens for many people."[9]

Outside the academy, coalitions, membership organizations, and business groups have taken up the cause. The 32 million-member American Association of Retired Persons (AARP) contends that "health care costs are out-of-control—and out of reach for many Americans."[10] Robert D. Ray, cochairman of the National Leadership Coalition for Health Care Reform, recently said "we have a very grave situation. We can't go on without doing anything."[11] The U.S. Chamber of Commerce has supported health care reform since 1971 and believes "important steps can and should be taken immediately to address the interrelated and apparently worsening problems of [health care] cost and access."[12]

While government is already a major presence in the health care industry, accounting for some 42 percent of health care spending, the high cost of health care is being used by some groups and individuals to justify still more intervention. Aaron at The Brookings Institution calls for empowering government agents "to establish and enforce payment schedules for physicians, . . . to negotiate hospital reimbursements, . . . to set fixed budgets as a means of controlling growth of hospital spending, . . . to stipulate services that would be paid for only if rendered in hospitals, and to specify which hospitals would receive payment for specified procedures."[13]

Enthoven and Kronick call for a "universal health insurance plan" that would require employers to provide insurance for all full-time employees or pay an 8 percent payroll tax, and create a system of "managed competition" involving tax-funded insurance programs and extensive government "monitoring" of health care providers. Physicians for a National Health Program, the National Leadership Coalition for Health Care Reform, and the AARP all support national health insurance, socialized medicine, or both.

It is tempting to agree with these academics, business leaders, and reform advocates that health care spending is too high. But it would be a serious mistake to agree with this statement without a careful examination of what it means. Agreement often constitutes acceptance of a rationale for determining the "right" level of spending. This rationale, in turn, supports specific reform agendas.

Even if we believe health care spending is in fact too high, it is valuable to ask how we know this and exactly what we mean by it. That is what this chapter is about.

When critics say the United States spends too much on health care, they typically point to spending on other goods and services, spending in earlier times, or spending in other nations to support their claims. Such comparisons, though, suffer four ways: They confuse cost with spending, they are hobbled by measurement problems, they are often irrelevant, and they disregard the inherent subjectivity of value.

Cost vs. Spending

In every country with national health insurance or socialized medicine, the level of health care spending is capped by government decree. But health care *costs* are not reduced by such caps. The reasons for health care spending remain, unmet, under a spending cap. The distinction between costs and spending is an important one, yet confusion of the two characterizes most attempts to measure health care spending.

The *cost* of any act is the most valuable alternative thereby forsaken.[14] The cost of buying a hamburger for $1.25, for example, is the value of whatever else could have been bought at that price plus whatever nonprice costs the purchase imposes (a long wait in line, for example). Cost includes not only the money price of a good or service, but also the time consumed by (or lost as a consequence of) the act and possibly time, money, and satisfaction lost by other people affected by the act.

Spending is price times the quantity of goods and services purchased. Whereas costs are always incurred when health care is produced, no spending occurs if that service is not bought or sold in a commercial market. For example, when a person has a cold and buys medication to relieve the symptoms, the money spent on the medication is recorded as spending on health care. If that person did not buy medication and instead chose to stay home from work for two days until the symptoms passed, no spending would be reported, yet a substantial cost would have been incurred. The cost would be lost wages borne by the individual and two days of a worker's production lost to the rest of society.

Why is this distinction important? First, because it reveals that spending levels bear no relationship to costs in countries whose governments determine the price and availability of health care. An accurate comparison of the cost of health care in the U.S. and Britain, for example, would require that we calculate for Britain the cost of pain, lost productivity, and sometimes the premature death of the 800,000 people in waiting lines to receive medical treatment each year. Nine thousand Britons, for example, die each year because they are denied access to kidney dialysis.[15]

Distinguishing cost from spending has other implications for health care comparisons. Many countries have not commercialized health care to the extent the U.S. has. Care is often provided in the home and/or by persons who do not report the payments they receive. Many health care costs in these countries therefore are not reported as spending.[16] The care of the elderly is an example of a health service that is commercialized in the U.S. but not in many other countries.

The increased commercialization of health care also explains some part of the increase in health care spending in the U.S. during the past two decades. During this period, prices were put on many costs that already were being incurred by family members or by patients. The tremendous increase in the number of people living in nursing homes has increased health care spending even though the cost of caring for the elderly may not have risen nearly as much.

Measurement Problems

A second reason it is difficult to determine whether spending on health care is "too high" is that we are ill-equipped to measure how much is being spent and how much is being bought.

The methodology for calculating Gross Domestic Product (GDP) varies from country to country, and in every country it is suspect. The literature admits that decisions on what to include in and exclude from national income accounts are often arbitrary.[17] For example, the salaries of all government employees are simply added together and then added to the estimate of GDP in the U.S., without regard to the value, if any, of their work. Activities that lower the quality of life, such as pollution, are not taken into account at all. The value of work you perform for yourself or your family is not counted, but when the same work is performed for someone else and compensated it *is* counted. Similarly, *barter* is not included in calculations of GDP. Since home treatment and barter are more likely to occur in countries where doctors' incomes are stringently controlled and services rationed, GDP underestimates costs in countries with nationalized health care.

The original source for most international comparisons using GDP—the U.S. Department of Health and Human Services (using data supplied by the Organization for Economic Cooperation and Development (OECD))—repeatedly cautions that estimates of international spending are "far from perfect" and that "individual countries are continually revising their underlying figures."[18] Some countries do not include nursing home spending in their estimates of health care spending.[19]

There is relatively limited international trade in services, further complicating comparisons. Even within a country, pricing *services* is more difficult than pricing commodities because differences in quality are more difficult to quantify. Attempts to take into account the changing value of health services have been particularly inadequate because of the rapid changes in technology, service delivery, and drug therapies. Despite dramatic increases in what could be called the "units of quality" of health care, measures of the cost of health services *assume that quality has remained largely unchanged.*[20] Stanford economist Victor R. Fuchs expressed it this way:

It is not easy to say how much of the increase in cost in

the past decade is due to the increased quantity of health care and how much to higher prices. Price should refer to some well-defined unit of service, but in fact the "content" of a physician's visit, or of a day in the hospital, keeps changing over time. . . . But because the official price index makes little allowance for changes in health care *quality* (i.e., the effects on health or the amenities associated with care) it may give a misleading picture of the true changes in *quantity.*[21]

Measurements that form the basis for GDP and other yardsticks used for international comparisons fail to account for changes in the quality of health services. As a result, they significantly overstate medical cost inflation over time and U.S. spending relative to spending in other countries.

Relevant Comparisons

Even if the methods of measuring health care costs and spending were accurate, the problem would remain of knowing when comparisons are relevant. Consider, for example, comparisons of health care spending to the Consumer Price Index (CPI). Such a comparison shows that health care prices between 1970 and 1990 rose 37 percentage points more than prices on all goods and services. (See Figure 1-2.)

But is the CPI a relevant standard for comparison? The CPI includes prices for durable goods, which rose at just half the pace of all prices from 1970 to 1990. A better comparison would be between prices for health care services and prices for other *services.* And even this comparison may not be particularly relevant because health care is a technology-intensive enterprise employing unusually well-educated people; it has more in common with higher education than, for example, janitorial and delivery services. Comparing the medical care price index to the higher education price index reveals that since 1970 medical care prices have risen 20 percentage points more than higher education prices, approximately half the difference found when the comparison was to the consumer price index. (See Figure 1-3.)

What of comparisons of U.S. health care spending this year to the amount spent in previous years? Such comparisons are

Figure 1-2. *Medical Care Price Index vs. Consumer Price Index, 1970-1990*

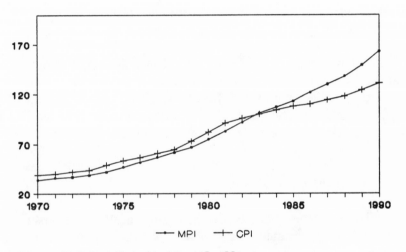

—•— MPI   —+— CPI

Source: Statistical Abstract of the U.S., 1991

constantly made in popular and scholarly articles. But unless we assume that the *reasons* for health care spending remained relatively unchanged over time, we cannot claim that spending levels in 1960 or even 1992 are relevant to the amount spent in 1993. If we cannot make the assumption, comparisons to past spending levels are irrelevant.

A review of health care spending patterns reveals that the reasons for spending have in fact changed over time. For example, the pregnancy rate for unwed teenagers rose from 12.6 to 31.6 per thousand between 1950 and 1985. Babies born to such mothers are far more likely to have low birth weights, and therefore to need more expensive medical interventions. Violent crime, drug-addicted babies, and AIDS were not health crises in 1960, but they are in the 1990s. Today's population is older and more likely to be Black American or Hispanic than was the population twenty years ago, and each of these groups is

Figure 1-3. *Medical Care Price Index vs. Higher Education Price Index, 1970-1989*

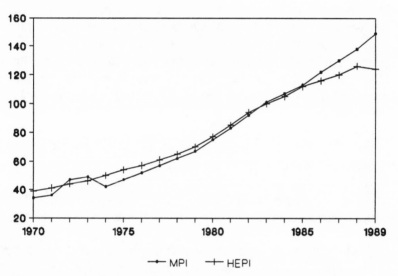

—•— MPI   —+— HEPI

Source: National Center for Education Statistics, Digest of Education Statistics, 1990; Statistical Abstract of the U.S., 1991.

characterized by greater health care needs. Government has pumped hundreds of billions of dollars into the health care industry since 1960, bidding up the price of doctors and other scarce health care inputs. The rise of the nursing home industry, changes in tort law that have led to multi-million dollar judgments against doctors and hospitals . . . Obviously, this list could go on.

Despite the fact that the marketplace for health care in 1993 is dramatically different than the marketplace was in 1960, comparisons continue to be made, and surprise is expressed that spending has grown so much since then. Why not instead imagine our surprise if the U.S. *were* able to care for its new elderly, its impoverished minorities, its AIDS victims and crack babies, and *not* spend dramatically more than it did in 1960?

If year-to-year comparisons are to be relevant, complex and

multitudinous changes over time must be measured and controlled. The difficulty of doing so for a single country, however, pales in comparison to the difficulties analysts face when attempting to make relevant *international* comparisons. Economist Joseph A. Pechman observed in 1958 that

> the conceptual problems become important when comparisons are made between countries or, for a single country, between periods that are far apart. For such comparison some attempt must be made to allow for the effect of changes in the scope of market activity, in the quality of output, and in institutional and business arrangements.[22]

For international comparisons to be relevant, social, economic, and cultural differences between two or more nations, each with its own way of defining and measuring data and each undergoing its own changes every year, must be measured and controlled. Researchers often are not even sure which factors to control.

Many European countries, for example, spend far less than does the U.S. on efforts to keep premature infants alive and extend the lives of the chronically ill elderly. Europeans have made different choices than have Americans, and these choices have resulted in different health care spending levels. The true cost of these decisions is only measurable in preventable deaths.

Similarly, the rights of patients in the U.S. are protected by a tort law system that pays billions of dollars to lawyers and dissatisfied patients each year. The cost of not protecting patients' rights includes lower-quality health care for future patients. Controlling for these often-subtle differences may not be possible, yet they undoubtedly challenge the relevancy of international comparisons.

Subjectivity of Values

A fourth problem with saying health spending is "too high"

is that such a statement overlooks the inherent subjectivity of values. The "data" for determining whether spending is too high are stored in the minds of the millions of consumers and providers who buy and sell health services. Their knowledge is simply not available to a single mind, and without it no judgment as to the "right" level of spending can be made.[23]

The subjectivity of values means no one can claim to speak for "society" when commenting on health care spending or any other topic involving the judgments of many other individuals. Each consumer increases the amount spent on a service until the value perceived from the last dollar spent is no less than the value expected from the best alternative. Putting a value on the last dollar spent is an internal and subjective process. The value is made public only when willing buyers and willing sellers agree to transact business at a particular price.

The subjectivity of values makes it difficult to speak of "social problems" or "national solutions." This difficulty has been spelled out in rigorous detail by a series of prominent economists including Ludwig von Mises[24] and Nobel Prize winners Friedrich Hayek[25] and James Buchanan.[26]

The subjectivity of values makes statements about health care spending especially difficult because so much of what is delivered by a health care system is felt only by individual patients.[27] Most people, for example, would pay several hundred dollars to avoid intense pain. Many diseases and illnesses impose greater injury and pain the longer treatment is delayed, so many of us would pay a premium for immediate treatment. Many of us also would pay more to stay in a private room rather than a ward, even though the higher expense is unlikely to affect any measurable outcomes of a medical procedure. Who, besides the individual patient, is to say whether the prices paid for these benefits are too high?

If one includes the subjective costs associated with the delivery of health care in other countries—longer waits and therefore greater suffering, greater pain during medical procedures, and longer recovery periods, for example—it is likely that many foreign countries have higher health care *costs* than does the U.S., even though their *spending* may be lower. Paying $1,000 in the

U.S. for a procedure that costs only $500 in Canada, for example, might be justified by the benefit of escaping a month, a week, or even a day sooner from pain. That the U.S. has reached a level of affluence that allows us to pay more to avoid pain is something to be admired, not criticized.

How We Know Spending is Too High

Acknowledging that values are subjective does not preclude us from reaching a judgment as to whether spending on health care is too high. In fact, understanding that values are subjective gives us the only true foundation for making such a judgment.

In an open and competitive marketplace, the "right" amount of spending on any good or service is simply the quantity purchased multiplied by the per-unit price charged. Prices are set by the interaction of supply and demand. When demand outstrips available supply, the price of the scarce product is bid up. The higher price attracts new suppliers into the market, resulting in a new balance of supply and demand. When demand lags behind supply, suppliers cut their prices to attract reluctant buyers. Suppliers produce less of the now less-profitable good, thereby lowering supply, resulting in a new supply and demand equilibrium at the lower price.

Figure 1-4 illustrates supply and demand in an imaginary market. Each point along the *demand curve*, labeled D1, represents the quantity of the product that consumers would purchase at a given price. For example, at price A, consumers would be willing to buy the quantity D. The demand curve slopes downward because as the per-unit price falls, the quantity people are willing to buy increases. The *supply curve*, labeled S1, represents the quantity of the product that suppliers would produce at each price. The supply curve slopes upward because suppliers are willing to produce more at higher prices. The intersection of the supply and demand curves represents the "market clearing" price—the price at which all of the good or service produced would be purchased. In our imaginary market, the market clearing price is B and the quantity purchased is C.

An individual's demand for health care behaves much like demand for other goods: It rises as price falls and falls as price rises.[28] But the supply of and demand for health care are heavily influenced by government policies.*

Figure 1-4. *Supply and Demand*

Price

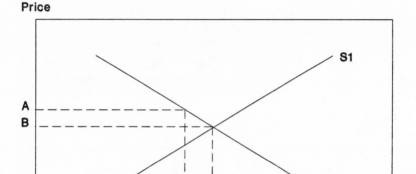

Several government policies increase the cost of supplying health care. State governments enforce some 700 laws mandating that insurance companies provide coverage for specified conditions. These mandates have been estimated to increase the cost of health insurance by 30 percent. Rules and regulations imposed on hospitals that accept Medicaid and Medicare payments are extraordinarily extensive and complex. Some of these regulations—among them the requirement that hospitals establish utilization committees to review the "appropriateness" of treatment provided—have been used by private insurers to limit their obligations to reimburse hospital costs. State governments also add

---

*These policies are discussed in greater detail in Chapter 4.

to the cost of health care by enforcing Certificate of Need requirements for new hospital construction, occupational licensing laws that prevent nurses and other health practitioners from performing many routine health care functions, and restrictions on managed care agreements reached between insurers and health care providers.

Government policies also increase the *demand* for health care and make demand less responsive to prices. The biggest single consumer of health care services in the U.S. is government, accounting for 42.4 percent of total health care spending. By spending hundreds of billions of dollars on health care each year, federal and state governments have increased the demand for health care services dramatically. Government tax policies further stimulate demand by encouraging employers to purchase low-deductible, low-copayment health insurance policies for employees. Persons with such insurance have little incentive to economize or comparison-shop because they are spending someone else's money whenever they enter the health care marketplace. The prices charged for health services do not matter to the consumer when an insurance policy covers the entire expense.

Figure 1-5 illustrates the effect of government policies on the supply and demand for health care. By imposing mandates and regulations that increase the cost of supplying health care, governments have shifted the supply curve for health services to the left (from S1 to S2) and made it rise more steeply. (The steeper upward slope means additional spending buys a smaller increase in the quantity of services delivered.) By spending billions of dollars on health care and encouraging reliance on low-deductible and low-copayment insurance policies, government policies have shifted the demand curve for health services to the right (from D1 to D2) and made its downward slope more steep. (The steeper downward slope means a given change in price results in a smaller change in the quantity of services demanded.) The new point of intersection for the supply and demand curves is at a higher price (E) and greater quantity (F) than would have prevailed in the absence of government intervention. The necessary result of government intervention, in other words, is to increase overall spending on health care.

The "right" level of spending for any good or service is the market-clearing price times the quantity sold at this price. In the health care marketplace, we know that both supply and demand

Figure 1-5. *Effect of Government Policies on Health Care Supply and Demand*

Price

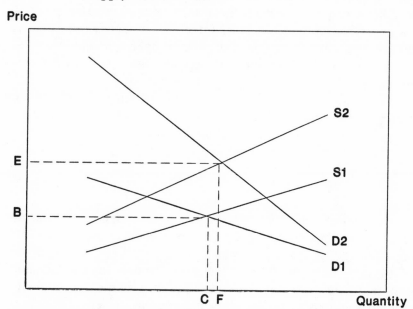

are heavily influenced by government policies. These policies tend to inflate demand and increase the cost of producing services, resulting in a higher level of spending than would prevail in the absence of government intervention. The current level of spending on health care, then, is not the "right" level: It is artificially high, a consequence of public policies rather than the actual interests of consumers and providers.

If tax laws treated out-of-pocket medical expenses as favorably as they treat employer-provided health insurance, the number of health care consumers who economize and comparison-shop would increase dramatically. The demand curve for health care would flatten. If insurance mandates and unnecessary regulations were repealed, the supply curve for health care would shift back to the right and rise less steeply. Both changes would lower total spending on health care by allowing supply and demand to reflect the true interests of health care consumers and suppliers.

The reform plans described in Chapter 6 would reduce the distorting effects of government spending, tax policy, and regulation on the health care market. It is certain that health care spending would fall substantially if such reforms were adopted, as consumers would begin to spend their own money on services that are now thought of as free, and suppliers would be freed from restrictions on the kinds of services and insurance policies they can offer.

Because we are certain spending would fall once people are given responsibility for their own health care spending decisions, *we know that current spending levels are too high.*

Policy Implications

To some readers, the preceding discussion may seem circular. We began by *rebutting* the evidence and arguments marshalled by critics who contend spending is too high, yet we end by *agreeing* with their assessment. There is no contradiction here: This exercise in accurate thinking helps us evaluate proposed solutions to the health care spending problem.

Let us say that we judge spending to be too high simply because spending in other countries is lower. Such countries have government-imposed caps on spending, and many health services available commercially in the U.S. are not available at all or are delivered by family members. To accept the comparison as relevant means either embracing these cost-control strategies or agreeing that the U.S. must find other means to reduce spending. But why should we do either? If we do not approve of these means, then comparisons of the spending levels they produce are irrelevant.

If the quality of health services is difficult to measure, and even more difficult to compare across nations, then international comparisons tell us very little about the quality of health care we would receive if we followed the lead of other nations. Is an office visit in Canada, Germany, or Britain as valuable as an office visit in the U.S.? Is a hospital stay more or less likely to result in quick relief from pain or an end to disability? If we cannot compare the quality of these services—and no reliable data have been cited by those who promote such international comparisons—then how can these comparisons tell us we would be satisfied with spending less?

By understanding the differences between cost and spending, the shortcomings of measurements of spending, and the factors that often make comparisons irrelevant, we can see through these misleading arguments to the real basis for determining the "right" level of spending on health care. If distortions in the market are responsible for unnecessarily high spending levels, then the only solution is to remove these distortions. Our success at bringing spending back to the "right" level will not be measured as a percent of GDP or by comparison to some previous year's spending, because neither of these measures is accurate, relevant, or consistent with the values of individual health care consumers. Rather, the right level of spending will be the amount spent by consumers in a competitive marketplace with minimum distortions imposed by government subsidies, regulations, and tax policies.

CHAPTER TWO

International Comparisons

DESPITE THEIR methodological defects, international comparisons are used widely to support arguments for a "comprehensive restructuring" of the health care industry. Such comparisons are said to document how spending in the U.S. is "out of control" and "rising faster than in any other nation,"[1] while other countries have been able to lower costs without compromising access to or the quality of care. Their achievement, the argument goes, is made possible by the fact that they have nationalized their health care systems. The final step in the argument is that spending in the U.S., too, could be controlled if only we followed the lead of other nations.

In fact, using their own numbers, we can show critics of the U.S. health care system that the U.S. has a *better* record of controlling spending than several developed countries that have adopted the nationalization model. This is remarkable given that the methods employed to collect such data are heavily biased against the U.S., and the U.S. faces far greater public health demands than do other developed nations.

The discussion that follows limits itself to international comparisons of *spending* because comparisons of *health levels* across nations tell us very little about the quality or efficiency of health care systems. To say, for example, that life expectancy is longer in Sweden than in the U.S. does not mean that health care in the U.S. is somehow deficient. *Health care* plays a very small role in determining such factors as longevity or infant mortality. As Victor Fuchs explains,

Today, however, differences in health levels between the United States and other developed countries or among populations in the United States are not primarily related to differences in the quantity or quality of medical care. Rather, they are attributable to genetic and environmental factors and to personal behavior. Furthermore, except for the very poor, health in developed countries no longer correlates with per capita income.[2]

Percent of GDP

The most common statistic used to measure health care spending in the U.S. is spending as a percent of Gross Domestic Product (GDP). Gross Domestic Product is an estimate of the total value of domestically generated wealth in a nation. Expressing spending as a percent of GDP gives an idea of what share of a nation's wealth is devoted to health care.

In 1990, health care expenditures constituted 12.1 percent of GDP in the U.S. This was higher than any other Western developed nation. In France, West Germany, and Canada, for example, health care spending was 8.8, 8.1, and 9.3 percent of GDP, respectively. By this measure, health care spending in the U.S. is high. (See Figure 2-1.)

Recent *trends* in spending also can be expressed in terms of percent of GDP. A study published by the University of Wisconsin in 1989 estimated that health care spending in the U.S. rose from 6.0 percent of GDP in 1965 to 11.1 percent in 1986, a much higher rate of increase than in other major countries.[3] Other sources also claim that U.S. spending by this measure is rising rapidly compared to other nations.[4]

The University of Wisconsin study is typical in that it presents an incomplete and inaccurate picture of health care spending trends. Simply beginning the analysis five years earlier than did the University of Wisconsin researchers—using data from 1960 (the first year data are available) through 1986—reveals that Japan and Italy increased health care spending as a percent of GDP faster than did the U.S. Figure 2-2 shows health care spending growth as a percent of GDP for eight countries.

Using percent-of-GDP to compare spending *trends* across countries is misleading when the countries being compared have different economic growth rates. Much of the increase in health

Figure 2-1. *Health Care Spending in 1990 as a Percent of GDP*

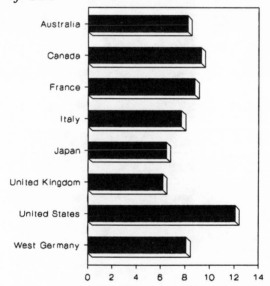

Source: Health Care Financing Review, Summer 1992, page 4.

care spending as a percent of GDP in the U.S. in the 1980s was caused by the slow growth of GDP, rather than by a rapid rise in health care spending. Indeed, between 1980 and 1985, the rate of health care spending growth in the U.S. fell sharply—to a level in 1985 that was lower than at any time since 1963. (See Figure 2-3.) Unfortunately, growth in GDP also was at historic lows, with the result that health care spending as a percent of GDP recorded a modest increase.

Differences in GDP growth for the U.S. and Canada are largely responsible for the mistaken belief that Canada has been more successful than the U.S. in controlling health care spending.

According to Edward Neuschler,[5] inflation-adjusted per-capita GNP[6] in Canada grew 74 percent between 1967 and 1987, while real growth in the U.S. was only 38 percent. This meant that,

Figure 2-2. *Growth in Health Care Spending as a Percent of GDP, 1960 to 1987*

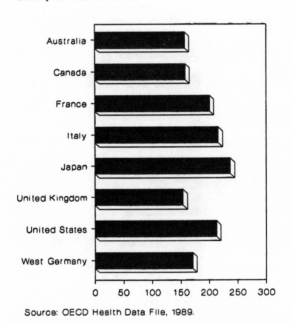

Source: OECD Health Data File, 1989.

even though the average annual increase in *per-capita spending* on health care rose slightly faster in Canada than in the U.S. (4.28 percent in Canada compared to 3.93 percent in the United States) during this period, U.S. spending as a percent of GDP rose faster than Canadian spending as a percent of GNP.

Per-capita Spending

Comparing health care expenditures on the basis of *per-capita* spending is only a small improvement over the percent-of-

GDP method. Per-capita spending is not obscured when economic growth rates differ, so the error made in the U.S.-to-Canada comparison described above is less likely to occur. When foreign currencies are converted into U.S. dollars using a purchasing power parity (PPP) index,[7] comparisons of the quality of health

Figure 2-3. *Annual Rate of Change in U.S. Health Care Expenditures*

Source: Health Care Financing Review, Summer 1992, page 18.

care purchased are nominally possible. But the many other measurement, relevancy, and subjectivity problems afflicting international comparisons remain. Henry Aaron, for example, does not use the PPP index "because this series depends on market prices for a small proportion of total health care spending in countries where most health care services are not marketed."[8] Since a larger proportion of health care spending in the U.S. is marketed than in other countries, spending levels in other countries are underestimated vis-a-vis U.S. spending.

Using the PPP index, we find again that health care

spending in the U.S. is considerably higher than in other countries. (See Figure 2-4.) Per-capita spending in the U.S. in

Figure 2-4. *Per-capita Health Care Spending, 1990, in U.S. Dollars, PPP-adjusted*

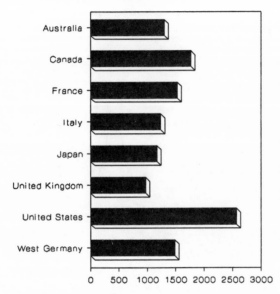

Source: Health Care Financing Review, Summer 1992, page 5.

1990 was $2,566, compared to $1,770 in Canada, $1,486 in West Germany, and $1,171 in Japan.

While the PPP index shows that U.S. spending is high relative to other nations, it also shows that spending by the U.S. has been high at least since 1960, and that *spending by other countries is increasing more rapidly than spending by the U.S.* In Figure 2-5, the change in per-capita spending on health care in seven countries from 1961 to 1990, measured as a percentage of U.S. per-capita spending, is illustrated.

Four countries—Japan, Italy, France, and West Germany— increased their per-capita spending relative to the U.S. between 1961 and 1990. Japan, for example, increased its spending from just 17.3 percent of U.S. per-capita spending in 1961 to 45.6 percent in 1990, an increase of 163 percent. Italy rose from 31.1

Figure 2-5. *Growth in Per-Capita Spending as a Percent of U.S. Spending, 1961-1990*

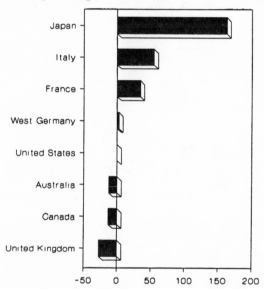

Source OECD Health Data Files, Health Care Financing Review, Summer 1992; Heartland Institute calculations.

percent to 48.2 percent, a rise of 55 percent. Three countries spent less, as a percentage of U.S. per-capita spending, in 1990 than they did in 1961: Australia (12 percent less), Canada (12 percent less), and Britain (27 percent less). Changes of just 12 percent over a thirty-year period can hardly be surprising, particularly in light of the social and economic changes experienced in each nation. Britain's drop of 27 percent relative to the U.S. stands out, but cultural and institutional factors described in the next chapter account for this anomaly.

The per-capita measure of health care spending shows U.S. spending is rising fifth fastest of eight countries, hardly a ranking that should cause alarm. Figure 2-6 illustrates how similar the spending patterns of the eight countries have been since 1961.

How We Compare

International comparisons do not reveal what advocates of spending constraints have told us to expect.

Figure 2-6. *Per-capita Health Care Spending as a Percent of U.S. Spending, 1961-1990*

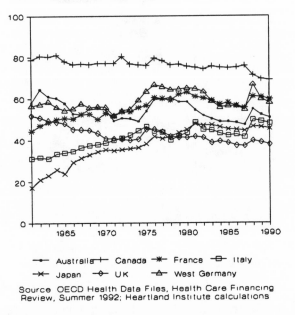

—•— Australia —+— Canada —✱— France —🗗— Italy
—✕— Japan —◇— UK —△— West Germany

Source OECD Health Data Files, Health Care Financing Review, Summer 1992; Heartland Institute calculations

Health care spending in the U.S. does appear to be high by international standards, both as a percent of Gross Domestic Product (GDP) and measured as per-capita spending using the purchasing power parity (PPP) index. However, two nations—Italy and Japan—increased their spending as a percent of GDP *faster* than did the U.S. from 1960 to 1987.

International comparisons of *per-capita* spending suggest a slower rate of spending growth by the U.S. Since 1960, four countries (Japan, Italy, France, and West Germany) have increased their health care spending faster on a per-capita basis than did the U.S. Australia and Canada increased their spending at a slightly slower rate than did the U.S., while only Britain's spending rose at a significantly slower rate.

The alleged inefficiency and waste of the U.S. health care system is not apparent from these comparisons. Missing, too, are the widely claimed economies and savings of the nationalized systems of Canada, Japan, Italy, and France.

In the following chapter we document how the need for health care spending in the U.S. has increased substantially over time and is significantly greater than in other nations. When we take these data into account, the U.S. record on health care cost containment compares favorably to the records of many other nations. This does not mean that spending in the U.S. is as low as it "should" be. As we noted earlier, the "right" spending level is still unknown, but it is almost certainly lower than current spending levels. Nevertheless, international comparisons *do* reveal that the U.S. health care system probably has controlled costs better than some of the nationalized systems of other countries. It has done so without resorting to the rationing and ethical compromises that are common in countries with nationalized health care.

CHAPTER THREE

Why Health Care Costs Are So High

THIS CHAPTER reviews the factors responsible for high health care costs in the U.S. While grappling with these challenges, the U.S. health care system has kept its rate of spending growth near or below the rates of six other developed nations to which the U.S. is routinely compared.

Wealth and Culture

The United States' high standard of living explains a great deal of its high health care spending relative to other nations. The higher a nation's income, the larger the share of personal income its citizens tend to spend on health care. The relationship holds true across national and cultural lines. The more money people have, the more they spend on their health.

According to conventional measures, the U.S. is the wealthiest nation in the world. (See Figure 3-1.) Per-capita GDP in the U.S. is 39 percent higher than in Japan, 38 percent higher than in West Germany, and 49 percent higher than in Britain. When per-capita GDP is compared to per-capita health care spending, a striking relationship emerges. This relationship, shown in Figure 3-2, has been closely studied.

According to health economist A.J. Culyer, "in 1971, a $100 increase in GDP per-capita could have been expected to increase health care expenditures by $8, or a 10 percent increase in GDP could have been expected to increase health care expenditures by about 13 percent."[1] Schieber and Poullier find that "each 10 percent difference in per-capita GDP is associated with a 14 percent difference in per-capita health spending."[2] The

Figure 3-1. *Per-capita Gross Domestic Product, 1990*

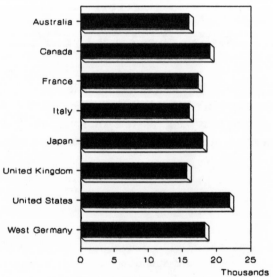

Source: Health Care Financing Review, Summer 1992.

Center for Health Policy Research of the American Medical Association estimates that a 10 percent increase in GDP is associated with a 20 percent increase in health care spending; thus, a $100 difference in per-capita GDP would equal an $18 difference in per-capita health care spending.[3] (This last estimate appears to be based on a smaller sample of nations.)

How much of the difference between U.S. and foreign per-capita health care spending can be explained solely by our higher level of income? According to Schieber and Poullier, the relationship explains $1,651—all but $400 of the $2,051 the U.S. spent per-capita on health care in 1987. Our higher GDP means we would spend $117 per person per year more than is spent in

Canada *even if* our health care systems were equally efficient and our populations and national public health statistics identical.

Figure 3-2. *Health Spending and Per-Capita GDP for 24 OECD Countries, 1987*

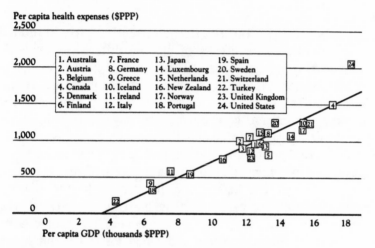

Reprinted by permission from *Health Affairs*, Fall 1989.
Source: Exhibit 3 and *National Accounts, Main Aggregates*, Volume 1 (Paris: OECD, 1989).

This analysis helps us make sense of international comparisons (if we hold in abeyance the many objections raised earlier to the meaningfulness of such comparisons). Very few people would want to see U.S. spending levels driven all the way down to the levels of Australia or Italy. It is useful for the purposes of spending analysis to say that $1,651 represents the level of U.S. per-capita spending on health care that would have prevailed in 1987 if differences in national income were "held constant."

Second only to our relative affluence, a uniquely American social and political culture seems to increase health care costs and drive health care spending. Lynn Payer has pointed out that standards of proper medical treatment vary substantially from country to country. The French, for example, typically report average hospital stays twice the length of those in the U.S., at least partly because they consider five weeks of vacation a year necessary for a healthy person to recuperate from a year's work.[4] West German patients consume more prescription drugs and see their doctors over twice as frequently as patients in France, Britain, or the U.S.

Payer's description of British health care standards dramatically illustrates the effects of cultural differences on health care costs and spending levels. "The British," notes Payer, "do less of nearly everything." Compared to Americans, British patients are half as likely to have surgery of any kind and one-sixth as likely to undergo coronary bypass surgery. British doctors prescribe fewer drugs, perform half the number of X-rays as U.S. doctors, and use half as much film per X-ray. Pap smears and blood tests are recommended only once every five years. The British do not treat for high blood pressure until the diastolic pressure is over 100, compared to 90 in the United States.[5]

Do the critics of U.S. health care believe we should adopt five-year intervals for pap smears and blood tests? Of course not. *But they compare U.S. spending to the spending of nations that have adopted such policies.* This invariably skews the results against the U.S. because, as Payer writes, "American medicine is aggressive. From birth—which is more likely to be by cesarean than anywhere in Europe—to death in a hospital, from invasive examination to prophylactic surgery, American doctors want to *do* something, preferably as much as possible."[6]

The consequences of this "aggressive" medical culture are pervasive. A one-year wait for a cataract operation is tolerated in Britain, but such a delay would result in a congressional investigation if it happened to a patient in the Veterans Administration system. Most Americans would find such delays unacceptable. This attitude has been ingrained by an economic system that enables Americans, more than the people of any other nation, to purchase goods and services without waiting in line. The U.S. has been able to avoid rationing health care or establishing queues because it allows people to pay a premium for

faster service. Having experienced such a responsive system,
Americans are understandably reluctant to give it up for systems
in which queues and service rationing are commonplace.

Hospitalization costs much more in the U.S. than elsewhere,
but the payoff is in shorter hospital stays. No country offers a
shorter length of stay than the U.S. In the Soviet Union and
China, it is more than twice as long. Even in Scandinavia,

Figure 3-3. *Average Length of Stay in Hospital*

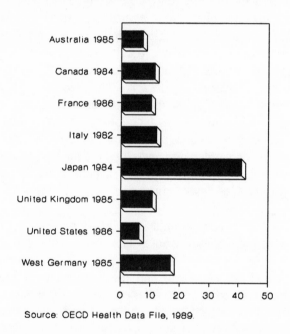

Source: OECD Health Data File, 1989.

hospital stays range from one to three days more than in the U.S.
for the same ailments—a significant percentage, since the average
U.S. hospital stay is now about 6.4 days.

In the U.S., providers administer prophylactic antibiotics and
other expensive drugs and promote early ambulation after surgery.
As a result, patients have speedier recoveries, quicker returns to
work, and reduced income loss.

Is this achievement necessarily better than longer stays in hospitals? Is the trade-off cost-effective? To answer these questions, we must know whether people in other nations would demand a similarly "aggressive" style of health care if their national health insurance system or socialized medicine did not prevent its delivery. We also need to know how much value patients place on returning home quickly after a medical procedure. In some cultures, longer convalescence may be a positive value; in the U.S. it is probably not. Once again our analysis is affected by the inherent subjectivity of values.

The American penchant for "aggressive" medicine is partly an unintended consequence of public policy. For example, our tort law system compels doctors to use the latest available technology or risk being sued by their patients. Cost containment strategies put in place under Medicare in 1983 are believed to have reduced the average length of stay in hospitals and increased the intensity of treatment and investments in technology. Heavy reliance on health insurance to pay medical expenses—a result of tax policy as well as genuine consumer demand—creates an environment that rewards doctors who perform surgery (perhaps even unnecessary surgery) and discourages less "aggressive" but also less expensive remedies.

Clyde McAvoy, a columnist for *Business Tokyo*, recently told of "an American friend whose Japanese wife needed open-heart surgery."[7] He took her to the U.S. for the operation. She was in the hospital for six days, and the surgery itself took two-and-one-half hours (compared to the estimated six hours for the same procedure in Japan). "Yes, the hospital and related care was expensive ($5,000 a day)," writes McAvoy, "but the point is that unfettered supply and demand assured availability of the hospital bed when she needed it and my friend's private insurance covered almost all the costs."

Did McAvoy's friend make the wrong decision?

Geography and Heterogeneity

The unique geography and demographics of the U.S. pose

special challenges for the task of organizing health care services not faced by other countries. While most Americans know that their country is larger, more populous, and more culturally and ethnically diverse than most other nations, few comprehend the magnitude of the differences or the impact they have on health care delivery.

A comparison of the U.S. to Sweden, the fourth largest nation of Europe (after Russia, France, and Spain), is instructive. (See Table 3-1.) Sweden has an unusually homogeneous population of 8.5 million people, 90 percent of whom live in densely settled areas in the southern third of the country. Ninety percent of Swedes belong to a single state church, and the nation has a common standard language. Sweden plans, organizes, and delivers health care services from a central agency with relative ease. Every element of health care delivery is controlled—from the size of a medical school class to hospital size and location, from budgets to hours of operation. There are no deep disagreements among ethnic or religious groups about medical ethics, service priorities, or institutional missions.

The United States, by contrast, has a population of more than 250 million spread over a continent. Its population is more than twice that of the second largest industrialized nation (Japan) and nearly 30 times that of Sweden. In physical area, the U.S. is 21 times the size of Sweden. It is difficult to imagine a single entity, public or private, attempting to make the sort of planning decisions made by Swedish health authorities.

The population of the U.S. is anything but homogenous. The U.S., unlike any other country in the world, is broadly multiracial (12 percent black, 7.6 percent Hispanic, and 80.4 percent white and others) and multireligious (57 percent Protestant, 28 percent Catholic, 2 percent Jewish, and 13 percent other or none). In the U.S., there is not one vision but many visions of what constitutes appropriate health care.

Comparing the population *density* of the U.S. to that of other countries also yields a useful insight. Health services, especially in a nation with an "aggressive" medical culture, must be provided at hospitals and clinics that are physically near their patients. If a country's population is spread out over large areas, more medical equipment and manpower are needed per capita to keep response and travel times low.

Table 3-1. *Comparing the U.S. to Sweden*

	Sweden	U.S.	U.S./ Sweden
Population (1990 proj.)	8.5 mill.	250.4 mill.	29.5
Area (square miles)	173,731	3.6 mill.	20.7
Religious Groups*	3	86	28.6
Ethnic Groups**	3	44	14.7

*Over 90 percent of Swedes belong to the state church. The U.S. figure represents the number of religious groups with memberships over 50,000.

**The U.S. figure represents the number of ethnic groups with memberships over 85,000, according to the 1980 U.S. Census.

Source: *Statistical Abstract of the U.S.*, 1989, 1991.

U.S. population density, in fact, is dramatically below that of most other countries to which we are routinely compared. (See Table 3-2.) The population density of Germany is 8.3 times that of the U.S.; Japan's density is 12.5 times as high. Of the eight nations we have been using for comparison, only Australia and Canada have lower overall population densities than the U.S. Both of these countries, however, are characterized by high population densities in small areas.

Decentralization, competition, and freedom of choice are the ways Americans have sought to serve so large and diverse a market. In health as in other fields, the freedom to organize into networks, corporations, and other entities is a celebrated American value. Hospitals, medical schools, and other health organizations in the U.S. have pluralistic ownership reflecting different health care philosophies, religious commitments, ethnic origins, and

Table 3-2. *Population and Population Density, 1990*

Country	Population (thousands)	Density	Country/US
Australia	16,923	6	0.1
Canada	26,538	7	0.1
France	56,358	267	3.8
Italy	57,664	496	7.2
Japan	123,642	860	12.5
U.K.	57,366	609	8.8
U.S.	250,410	69	---
Germany	78,475	570	8.3

Population = 1990 estimate; density = persons per square mile

Source: *Statistical Abstract of the U.S.*, 1991.

educational missions. Choice and competition among these different groups make it unnecessary to impose on a disparate people a single philosophy or method of practice. Appreciation for variety in the organization and management of hospitals and clinics dates back to the earliest years of the republic.

The enormous size and diversity of the American marketplace has given rise to a decentralized and competitive system of financing and delivering health care. Such a system necessarily has costs not incurred by systems operating in smaller, more dense, and more homogenous countries. To criticize this system for having these costs, then, is disingenuous. It assumes an unachieved and unachievable "ideal": a U.S. health care system run like the Swedish or German systems. Reality never compares well with utopian visions, and health care is no exception.

Sex, Crime, and Disease

Americans lead lifestyles that expose them to much higher rates of disease and health complications than faced by the people of most other nations. Sometimes we deliberately kill ourselves (see Figure 3-4)—suicide is the third leading cause of death among teenagers and young adults—but more often we eat, smoke, drink, or couch-potato ourselves to death. "It cannot be overemphasized," said former Secretary of Health and Human Services Louis W. Sullivan, "that the top ten causes of premature death in our nation are significantly influenced by personal behavior and lifestyle choices."[8]

We have ample reason to believe that American health habits are getting worse over time. Comparing data collected in 1977 and 1983, researchers found more obesity, less exercise, more drinking, and less sleep in 1983.[9] The prevalence of heart disease, high blood pressure, and limitation of activity due to disability is increasing. Infant mortality rates, known to be influenced by the lifestyles of pregnant women, long have been high by European standards. Who would have thought, one hundred years ago, that *obesity* would one day be the principal nutritional problem facing the United States?

Nicholas Eberstadt, a visiting fellow at the Harvard Center for Population Studies, says "data strongly suggest that habits, behaviors, and lifestyle arrangements that are characteristically American may be contributing powerfully to our high infant mortality rate. Changing them would improve our performance."[10] The unhealthy effects of habits and lifestyle also have been observed among the elderly in the United States after the introduction of Medicare and among the general populations of Eastern Europe after the introduction of public health services.[11]

Poverty is another cause of higher health care costs. Because they are often uninsured, low-income people with health problems often enter the medical system without prior notice through the emergency wards. Costs in emergency wards are considerably above those for general hospital admission and walk-in clinics. The poor often postpone getting treatment until symptoms reach high levels of discomfort or pain, with the result that treatment is often more time-consuming and expensive.[12]

Mortality rates among the poor historically have been high, but not because access to care is limited. Research in Britain and even in egalitarian Scandinavia confirms that mortality rates are

Figure 3-4. *Death Rate by Suicide in the U.S., 1960-1989 (per 100,000 population)*

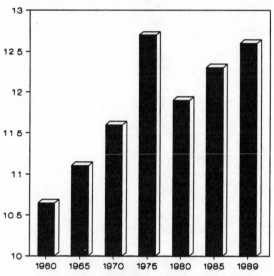

Source: Statistical Abstract of the U.S., 1988, 1989, 1991.

highest for families with the lowest incomes, even though access to health care is "free."[13] Leonard Sagan writes:

> Social class is strongly associated with the morbidity and mortality rates of a broad range of diseases and accidents. These differences in health have been persistent throughout this century. They affect children as well as adults and are almost certainly not the result of differences in access to medical availability.[14]

A particularly vexing problem confronting the health

profession in the U.S. is the growing number of births to unwed teenage mothers. (See Figure 3-5.) The U.S. teenage pregnancy rate is almost 2.5 times that of Canada and Britain. More prone to premature birth and the illnesses of poverty, these mothers and newborns require more extensive medical care than older, married women and their children.

Figure 3-5. *Pregnancies per 1,000 Women Age 15-19*

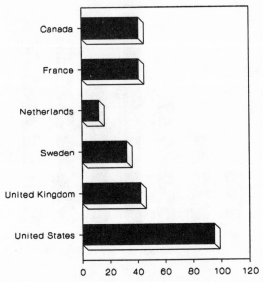

Source: Leonard Sagan, The Health of Nations: True Causes of Sickness and Well-Being, page 107.

Violent crime in the U.S. further contributes to health care costs. (See Figure 3-6.) Violent crime rates are much higher in the U.S. than in other countries. The U.S. male homicide rate, for example, is more than 12 times that of West Germany and five times that of Canada.[15] In an average year, Japan (population 120 million) experiences fewer than 2,000 homicides, robberies, and rapes. The U.S., with approximately twice the population, witnessed 629,000 such crimes in 1987, over 300 times the number in Japan. Most violent crime victims are treated in emergency rooms, where the costs are extremely high.

Drug use is another problem having a tremendous impact on U.S. hospitals and health care providers.[16] The National Association of Public Hospitals, representing the 100 largest government hospitals in the country, reported in January 1991 that

Figure 3-6. *Homicide Rate in U.S. (per 100,000 population)*

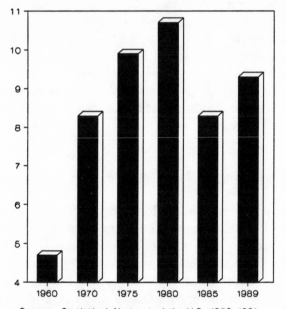

Source Statistical Abstract of the U.S., 1989, 1991

29 percent of all emergency room visits involved illegal drugs. On average, each hospital delivered 104 babies born addicted to cocaine each year.[17] The Drug Abuse Warning Network estimates that emergency rooms across the country had 426,060 drug-related visits in 1989 and 365,708 in 1990.[18]

There are approximately 375,000 "drug-exposed" infants in the U.S. Estimates for the cost of their treatment range from $500 million[19] to nearly $5 billion a year.[20] This problem is negligible in Canada and most other countries.

The AIDS epidemic is still another challenge that is

weighing more heavily on the U.S. health care system than on the systems of other nations. There are 100,000 AIDS patients in the U.S. and an additional 200,000 reported cases of HIV infection. The rate of incidence of AIDS in the U.S. in 1989 was more than three times that of Canada and six times that of West Germany. Treating AIDS is expensive: $85,000 during the lifetime of each patient and an estimated cost in 1991 of $5.8 billion.[21] One estimate projects the AIDS epidemic in the U.S. will have cost $12 billion—1.6 percent of total health care spending—in 1992.[22]

To our knowledge, none of the international comparisons of health care spending takes these lifestyle differences into account. Yet one cannot enter a hospital or talk to a physician in the U.S. without being struck by how many resources are invested in responding to poor health habits and the medical needs of the poor, unwed teenage mothers, the victims of violent crimes, drug users, and AIDS patients.

The Beginning and End of Life

In the U.S., extensive efforts are made to rescue premature infants. Many hospitals have state-of-the-art neonatal intensive-care units for premature and at-risk babies. There is a clear policy, supported by medical ethics as well as legal precedent, of making every possible effort to save viable infants. Saving one extremely premature baby costs approximately $158,000, and the nation spends an estimated $2.6 billion annually on neonatal intensive care.[23] Partly as a consequence of this commitment, nearly all of the advancements made in recent years in the care of extremely premature infants have come from U.S. health care institutions.

Other countries do not make this same commitment. "Swedish doctors tend to withhold treatment from the beginning from infants for whom statistical data suggest a grim prognosis," according to the Hastings Center Report.[24] "The British are more likely to initiate treatment, but withdraw it if the infant appears likely to die or suffer severe brain damage. The trend in the U.S. is to start treating any baby who is potentially viable and continue until it is virtually certain that the infant will die."

Despite this commitment, the U.S. infant mortality rate, at 11.0 per thousand population in 1988, is the highest among Western industrialized countries. Canada's rate, in contrast, was just 7.0 per thousand.[25] This statistic invariably appears in calls for reforming the U.S. health care system. Yet there is little relationship between infant mortality rates and health care spending or the organization of health care delivery.[26] The heroic efforts of doctors and nurses to save at-risk infants in the U.S. are overwhelmed by the effects of the mother's age, condition of health, and genetic background.

A 1979 study by the Department of Health, Education, and Welfare attributes only 10 percent of premature deaths in developed countries to inadequate health care services.[27] The balance are due to unhealthy lifestyles (50 percent), environmental factors (20 percent), and human biological factors (20 percent). More recent studies conducted by the National Center for Health Statistics have linked low birth weights for American babies with illegitimacy and maternal smoking, both thought to be proxies for a complex of attitudes and practices by parents that bear on the well-being of the baby.[28]

Right or wrong, defensible or not, other countries have adopted strategies to limit health care spending on premature infants. The U.S. has not, and as a result it spends far more than other countries on this group of patients. Those who claim that health care spending in the U.S. should be lower rarely acknowledge that legal and ethical decisions such as this underlie some of the cost differences observed among nations.

The gradually aging population of the U.S. is another key factor in rising health care spending. The proportion of the U.S. population that was 65 years or older rose from 9.2 percent in 1960 to 12.2 percent in 1987. By 2010 the figure is expected to be 13.9 percent. (See Figure 3-7.) The U.S. is currently in the middle of the range of other nations, with Canada and Japan having lower proportions (about 11 percent) and Britain and West Germany the highest (over 15 percent).[29]

The elderly are much more likely than are younger people to experience arthritis and rheumatism, heart conditions, hypertension without heart involvement, impairments of the lower extremities and hips, impairments of the back or spine, visual impairments, and emphysema. About 5 percent of the elderly in the U.S. reside in nursing homes.

Figure 3-7. *Percent of U.S. Population 65 Years or Older*

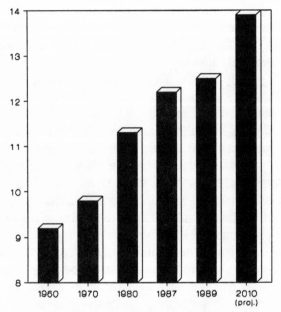

Source: Statistical Abstract of the U.S., 1989, 1991.

The average number of physician visits increases directly with age, and the rate of increase accelerates as one gets older. Persons 65 or older in 1985 averaged two visits per year more than those under the age of 45 (6.4 vs. 4.4), and their length of stay in hospitals (per admission) averaged 10.6 days versus 7.6 for the population as a whole.[30] Not surprisingly, the cost of health care for a person 65 or over is high: 3.9 times that of someone under 65.[31] Almost 30 percent of Medicare outlays for hospital care occur within the last year of patients' lives.[32]

In the Netherlands, gravely ill patients are given the option of euthanasia; government in Britain rations health care in part by providing services such as kidney dialysis and hip replacement only to persons below certain ages. Such care-limiting decisions, made implicitly or explicitly, have been accepted in countries where health care has been nationalized. In the U.S., however, huge sums of money are expended for care that is unavailable or withheld in other countries.

According to Victor Fuchs, the U.S. spends 1 percent of GNP on health care for elderly people in the last year of their lives[33]—over $45 billion in 1987 alone. Jacques Kransy and Ian R. Ferrier estimate that if Canada had the same elderly population as does the U.S. (as a percentage of total population), Canadian health care spending would be 5.3 percent higher than it is today.[34]

Once again we have identified a factor that influences health care in the U.S. far more significantly than in other countries. And again, the advocates of lower health care spending are strangely quiet about whether a new health care system would continue to meet the ethical standards met by the current one. Should medical services to the elderly be limited, regardless of their willingness and ability to pay for treatment? Other countries have answered "yes" to this question; the U.S. has said "no."

Technology and Law

The U.S. leads the rest of the world in the development and use of medical technology. The U.S. discovers new technologies, brings them to market, puts them to use across the country, and exports them to the rest of the world. Backed by government, private industry, and charitable gifts, the U.S. budget for health research and development dwarfs that of other nations.

A recent comparison of selected medical technologies in use in the U.S., Canada, and West Germany found the U.S. far ahead in both the number of units and their ratio to population. (See Table 3-3.) Compared to Canada, for example, the U.S. has (per-capita) nearly eight times more magnetic resonance imaging (MRI) and radiation therapy units, six times more lithotripsy centers, three times more cardiac catheterization and open-heart

surgery units, and slightly more organ transplant units.[35]
In 1990, the U.S. medical device industry enjoyed a $2.1 billion trade surplus and accounted for 48 percent of the entire

Table 3-3.   *Comparative Availability of Selected Medical Technologies*

	Canada (1989)			Germany (1987)			United States (1987)		
	Number of units	Persons per unit (1,000)	Units per million persons	Number of units	Persons per unit (1,000)	Units per million persons	Number of units	Persons per unit (1,000)	Units per million persons
Open-heart surgery	32	813	1.23	45*	1,355*	0.74*	793	307	3.26
Cardiac catheterization	39	667	1.50	161	379	2.64	1,234	198	5.06
Organ transplantation	28	929	1.08	28*	2,178*	0.46*	319	764	1.31
Radiation therapy	14	1,857	0.54	191	319	3.13	967	252	3.97
Extracorporeal shock wave lithotripsy	4*	6,500*	0.16*	21	2,904	0.34	228	1,069	0.94
Magnetic resonance imaging	12*	2,167*	0.46*	57	1,070	0.94	900	271	3.69

*1988.

Reprinted by permission from *Health Affairs*, Fall 1989.

world output of such equipment.[36] Because other countries contribute only a negligible amount to health technology development, they get the benefits of innovation without having to bear the R&D costs. A New Zealand health care executive put it this way: "We buy a great deal of U.S. technology, but we wait several years to see how it works out. Then, if it is good and economical, we buy it."

The "free ride" provided by U.S. R&D efforts brings sizable savings to other nations. According to one estimate, if Canada spent as much on R&D as does the U.S., its health care spending would be 2.4 percent higher than it is today.[37]

Meanwhile, the U.S. consumer demands—and legal

considerations often require—the ready availability of the latest diagnostic and therapeutic hardware, even before economies of scale or competition can bring the price down. Such technology has prolonged life, reduced inpatient admissions and length of stay, and dramatically improved the practice of medicine. It also has increased cost: A study of hospital costs between 1977 and 1983 estimated that half of the increase in real hospital costs was a result of technological investment and implementation.[38]

In part to manage their sophisticated equipment, hospitals demand and teaching hospitals produce doctors trained in specialties. These doctors tend to be higher paid and to work fewer hours than general practitioners. They also indirectly raise health care costs; as Victor Fuchs points out, "by virtue of their training, knowledge, inclination, and interests, specialists tend to order more services."[39]

Does the U.S. spend *too much* on technology? Do Canada and Germany spend too little? Here there appears to be no answer. In the U.S., the adoption of new technology is based on market decisions, but the market has been badly distorted deliberately as well as accidentally by the legal system, government regulation, and other government interventions. In Canada and Germany, decisions to limit investment in technology are made directly by government officials. Their decisions are based on political considerations that tend to trade long-term investments in capital for short-term labor support. It is possible, as one researcher has said, that "all levels could be optimal for the countries concerned, given different social values for technology in each."[40] What *is* certain is that technology makes medicine more expensive in the U.S. than in other countries.

The U.S. legal system also plays a role in rising health care costs, a phenomenon not experienced in most other countries. For example, U.S. courts establish "standards of care" that, until recently, were based on the state-of-the-art achieved in the local community. When a lawsuit was tried, a physician's judgment was generally compared to the opinions of other doctors in the local community.

Today, state-of-the-art comparisons are based on *national* standards. Technological breakthroughs in Boston are soon expected to reach Des Moines, Tupelo, and Cheyenne. Pressure for MRI units, fetal-monitoring equipment, and scores of other expensive tests and procedures is felt everywhere, intensified by articles in the popular press. The courts have played a key role in forcing a more rapid dissemination of new health-related technology than would otherwise take place.[41] The necessary result of this higher quality of care is higher costs.

The ever-present threat of lawsuits also has resulted in extremely high malpractice insurance premiums in the U.S. According to the General Accounting Office, "on average, premiums paid by self-employed Canadian physicians were less than one-tenth those paid by U.S. physicians." Canadian physicians are only one-fifth as likely to be sued for malpractice as U.S. physicians.[42] A 1993 study by Lewin-VHI, a health benefits consulting firm, estimated that doctors and hospitals paid $10 billion in direct medical malpractice insurance premiums in 1991, and that this cost would rise to $15 billion in 1998.[43]

High insurance premiums and the threat of lawsuits have compelled many doctors and hospital administrators to conduct tests, keep records, and perform medical procedures that would be unnecessary in a less litigious environment. "Defensive medicine" —taking every possible precaution against lawsuits from dissatisfied patients—has become a costly form of malpractice prevention. It has even invaded the classroom, where medical school students are being taught defensive medicine techniques. Lewin-VHI estimates that consumers would save between $36 billion and $78 billion over a five-year period if defensive medicine were reduced.[44]

An international counterpart to the U.S. malpractice crisis is difficult, if not impossible, to find. Many nations have difficulty even understanding the *concept* of malpractice; it just doesn't exist in many countries.

The U.S. legal system of contingency fees and large punitive awards also encourages the filing of lawsuits that would not be filed in another country. In most of the rest of the world, the *losers* in a legal battle must pay the legal fees of both sides. Such a policy discourages nuisance suits.[45] Over 80 percent of the lawsuits filed against hospitals and doctors in New York were found to be without foundation in a recent study of malpractice by Harvard Medical School researchers.[46] Ironically, efforts by doctors to discipline each other also are interfered with by the U.S. legal system. Disciplinary measures taken by hospital boards often are met with litigation alleging libel, wrongful discharge, and the like.

It can be argued (by lawyers if no one else) that the billions of dollars spent on malpractice insurance, litigation, and defensive medicine are not entirely, or perhaps even largely, wasted. Important benefits result from a legal system that allows patients to be reimbursed if they are harmed and victims to present the specific merits of their own cases. These cases may generate precedents that lower the cost of future litigation or deter behavior that may be harmful.[47] The tort system operates, albeit expensively, as a quality-control and accountability mechanism.

Can We Change?

Why is health care spending in the U.S. so high? One reason is that it *costs* a great deal to meet some of our unique needs. Rather than assume that high spending is necessarily bad or the result of a dysfunctioning health care system, the underlying *need* for health care spending must be explored. Our analysis finds that in the U.S.:

■ Our relatively high income compared to other nations is responsible for most of our higher health care spending.

■ We receive a more "aggressive" style of health care that translates into greater investments in technology, drugs, and surgery, and short hospital stays and waits for care.

■ Our large and heterogeneous population and relatively low population density make "streamlining" or centralizing the management of health care very difficult.

■ Our lifestyles are less healthy and much more dangerous than those of our foreign counterparts, placing a greater burden on our health care industry.

■ Doctors, patients, and those who shape the law have decided that premature and at-risk babies should be saved; such babies are allowed to die in most other nations.

■ A commitment also has been made to extend and make more comfortable the lives of our elderly, even at great cost.

■ Large investments are being made in research, development, and dissemination of new life-saving technologies; other nations "free ride" on our investment.

■ Tort law has changed to allow people who believe they have received inadequate care to file lawsuits and sometimes win large awards.

This list also can be read as a series of dilemmas facing Americans. Are we willing to limit health care spending if the price is waiting lines, longer recoveries, and lower odds of surviving a surgical procedure? Can we reduce teenage pregnancy, homicides and suicides, or drug abuse? Should we "streamline" the health care industry by limiting the variety of health care philosophies and methods of practice that can be offered and by restricting the choices available to consumers? Should we reconsider our commitment to premature infants and the elderly?

To suggest that public health problems account for much of health care spending in the U.S. is to invite the response, "But we can't do anything about those things." For several reasons, this response is wrong.

The nation's public health problems *can be* combated with effective education programs and the efforts of voluntary organizations such as Alcoholics Anonymous and Narcotics Anonymous. Many programs addressing nutrition, sex, and personal responsibility can influence school-age children, diminishing the odds that they will be heavy health care users in the future. Public policy changes hold some promise to reduce the rate of violent crime, litigation, and even teenage pregnancy. The time and effort that is now devoted to the "comprehensive restructuring" of the nation's health care system could be applied instead to the real causes of high health care spending.

The purpose of this exercise is not to prove that health care costs and health care spending cannot be reduced. It is, instead, to demonstrate that responsibility for doing so cannot be put entirely on the shoulders of insurers or health care providers. Even if we implement national health insurance or socialized medicine, there still will be crack babies, teenage pregnancies, lawsuits, and myriad other explanations for the high costs that plague the U.S. health care system.

CHAPTER FOUR

Why We Spend Too Much

IN ADDITION to factors that drive health care costs by increasing the real need for higher spending, there are other factors that cause "too much" spending. They arise from government subsidies, tax policy, and regulations.

Government Subsidies

It could hardly be surprising that government intervention plays a substantial role in health care cost inflation. State and federal governments spent over $280 billion on health care in 1990, up from just $24.9 billion in 1970. (See Figure 4-1.) Government spending accounted for 42.4 percent of total health care spending in 1990, a level higher than in any previous year. This massive spending increased demand for health care, resulting in a higher quantity of services delivered at higher prices.

The manner in which government funds are spent on health care also fuels health care inflation. For example, Medicaid beneficiaries make only small payments toward their medical expenses, giving them an incentive to overuse health services and little incentive to comparison-shop for lower-cost therapies or providers. Prior to 1983, health care providers were paid the estimated cost of the service plus an agreed-upon profit. This "cost-plus" pricing encouraged providers to expand the range and volume of services they delivered and increase the prices they billed the government.

The health care industry expanded dramatically in the 1970s

and 1980s to accommodate the influx of government spending. The number of doctors rose from 151 per 100,000 population in

Figure 4-1. *Government Spending on Health Care, 1970-1990*

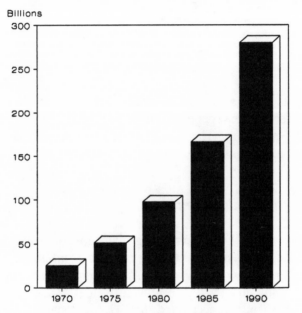

Source: Statistical Abstract of the U.S., 1991.

1970 to 246 by 1986.[1] The number of other hospital personnel increased from 2.53 million in 1970 to 3.46 million in 1986.[2] Heavy investments were made in capital and new technology, investments some critics contend would not have been made in a more cost-conscious environment. While studies of "unnecessary" hospitalizations, procedures, and medications are controversial,[3] most observers agree that consumers and providers both bear some responsibility for the two decades' rapid spending increases.

With its huge market share, changes in the federal government's reimbursement policy are immediately felt by other players in the health care field. The cost-plus payment system under Medicare forced other health care buyers, who bid against Medicare for health services, to pay higher prices. The heavy traffic of consumers for whom health care was nearly or entirely "free" made it more difficult for those consumers who were still cost-conscious to have any effect on prices.

Serious cost-containment efforts finally started in 1983, when the federal government changed Medicare reimbursement policies from cost-plus to predetermined payments for medical procedures grouped into diagnosis related groups (DRGs). Direct government financing of capital spending continued, with the federal government assuming 80 percent of capital costs.

Hospitals reacted to DRGs by changing the kind of care they delivered and attempting to shift costs. Hospitals increased the intensity of care by increasing per-patient staffing levels and taking an even more aggressive approach to treatment, thereby shortening the time patients spent in hospitals and allowing greater use of less-expensive out-patient care. Health statistics bear this out: Hospital occupancy rates (average daily census per 100 beds) were almost unchanged between 1975 and 1983, but then fell in each of the following years. (See Figure 4-2.) The number of "inpatient-days" fell by 17 million in 1984 alone.[4] Rising intensity was a trend well before the introduction of DRGs, but the trend clearly escalated during this period.

Starting in 1986, hospitals began shifting the cost of treating Medicare and Medicaid patients onto patients with private health insurance. Jack Meyer, Sharon Silow-Carroll, and Sean Sullivan describe the results:

> As Medicare and Medicaid have tightened their payment policies, providers have naturally tried to shift some costs to private payers. This cost shifting may not cause total health care spending to be any higher, but it increases the tab for many private employers and individuals. Insurers attribute 30 percent of the increase in employers' benefit costs for 1989 to cost shifting from these public programs. Additional cost shifting occurs when the uncompensated cost of providing care for the uninsured or medically indigent results in higher prices to private payers.[5]

Government's entry into the health care marketplace has

dramatically expanded the volume, intensity, and price of health care. By first bidding up the price of health care with a payment system that encouraged excessive utilization and spending, and

Figure 4-2. *Hospital Occupancy Rates, 1975-1988*
(per 100 beds)

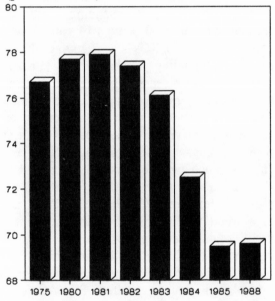

Source: Statistical Abstract of the U.S., 1989, 1991.

then imposing cost-containment measures that led to cost-shifting, government inadvertently has increased the cost of health care to other buyers and changed the way care is delivered. In so doing, government has contributed to a process that has priced health care and insurance out of the reach of millions of Americans.

Medicare and Medicaid *have* given the elderly and poor greater access to health care. However, this benefit must be weighed against the costs borne by taxpayers and other health care consumers. The manner in which this access has been attained produced substantial unnecessary costs. Later, we will examine policy alternatives that can retain the benefits of greater access without imposing unnecessary costs on other parties.

Taxation of Health Insurance Premiums

The second way government influences the price of health care is through its tax policies regarding health insurance.[6] Under current law, employers deduct the cost of health insurance premiums from their employees' *pre-tax* income, so one dollar of earned income buys one dollar's worth of health insurance. This arrangement gives persons with employer-paid health insurance a significant benefit compared to those without such insurance. When an employee pays directly for health care—because he or she is not insured, is self-insured, or is paying a deductible or copayment—the payment is made with *after-tax* income.

The impact of tax policy on health care spending is not insignificant. Employer and employee Social Security taxes (15.3 percent), federal income taxes (15-28 percent), and state and local income taxes (approximately 8 percent) can reduce one dollar of pre-tax income to 50 cents or less of post-tax income. Paying for health care with post-tax dollars, then, requires earning one dollar to buy 50 cents' worth of service. Having an employer purchase a health insurance policy, on the other hand, means a dollar's worth of earnings buys an entire dollar's worth of insurance.

The unequal treatment of employer-provided insurance vis-a-vis self-insurance or out-of-pocket expenditures on health care has increased reliance on employer-provided health insurance. The share of health care spending paid by business increased from 17 percent in 1965 to 28 percent in 1987, while the share paid directly by individuals fell from almost 90 percent in 1930 to just 25 percent in 1987.[7] (See Figure 4-3.) In 1985, 90 percent of the privately insured population obtained its insurance from employers or unions.[8]

Reliance on insurers has created a health care marketplace where individual consumers usually do not spend their own money. Even though insurance rates rise when medical costs rise, the conduct of any one patient does not have a significant impact on overall costs. Each individual with insurance, consequently, has an incentive to overuse medical services and no incentive to comparison-shop. In such a market, hospitals and other care providers are free (or *were* free, before the widespread adoption

of "managed care" programs) to over-serve and over-charge for
their services. Louise B. Russell, then of The Brookings
Institution, described the situation in these terms:

Figure 4-3. *Percent of Health Care Expenditures Paid Out of
Pocket, 1930-1987*

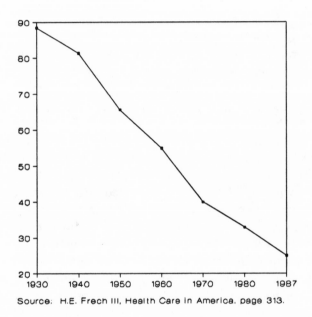

Source: H.E. Frech III, Health Care in America. page 313.

This incentive structure means that at the point at which
decisions are made about the use of resources, the people
who make those decisions are able to act as if the resources
are free. Rationally they can and do make decisions that
bring little or no benefit to the patient, since the resource
costs of the decisions—to the people making them—are also
little or nothing. And because of the extent to which
decisionmaking is shared in medical care, decisions can be
made that bring no benefit to the patient or even harm him,
if they bring benefits to someone else involved in making
the decisions. These benefits may come in the form of more

employment in hospitals, higher incomes for medical professionals, or research or teaching opportunities. In sum, there are virtually no economic constraints left to prevent decisionmakers in medical care from doing everything they can think of, no matter how small the benefits nor to whom they accrue; in economic jargon, they are free to head straight for the satiation point. In a complex area like medical care, that point is a distant and moving target.[9]

Little comparative information about the quality and price of medical procedures is now made available to consumers simply because consumers do not demand such information. Bills bear little relationship to the actual costs of services because hospitals are at liberty to subsidize their research, teaching, charitable care, or other loss-generating activities by charging more for routine procedures. The widely varying prices charged by hospitals in Illinois, for example, are revealed each year in a survey conducted by the Illinois Health Care Cost Containment Council. The survey found in 1990 that cataract removal ranged in price from $5,674 to $650, hernia repair from $4,329 to $404, and mammograms from $178 to $35.[10]

Beyond encouraging more people to rely on health insurance, favorable tax treatment of employer-provided insurance also has changed the kinds of insurance policies people buy. Low deductibles or first-dollar coverage, coverage of a wide range of optional medical procedures, and limited copayments are made economical when the much higher insurance premiums are paid by employers with pre-tax dollars. The results are much higher administrative costs (for handling very small claims), further incentives for consumers to overuse medical services, and still less incentive for consumers to monitor the prices of services they receive.

How significant is the effect of lower copayment rates on health care consumption and spending? Some idea can be gathered from a $136 million study conducted between 1974 and 1982 for the U.S. Department of Health and Human Services by the Rand Corporation.[11] The study, which involved 5,809 people at six sites around the country, varied copayment rates and the maximum dollar expenditure a family made each year. The study's results are summarized in Table 4-1.

Table 4-1. *Effects of Different Coinsurance Rates (CR):*
The Rand Study

Predicted Annual Per-Capita
Use of Medical Services, By Plan

Plan	Likelihood of Any Use	One or More Admissions to Hospital	Medical Expenses (1984 dollars)
Free Care	86.7%	10.37%	$777
25% CR	78.8	8.83	630
50% CR	74.3	8.31	583
95% CR	68.0	7.75	534

Source: David Greenberg and Mark Shroder, *Digest of the Social Experiments* (Madison, WI: Institute for Research on Poverty, Special Report No. 52, May 1991), page 197.

The Rand study found that copayment size had a significant effect on utilization of health services, number of hospital admissions, and annual medical expenses. The average person covered by a 50 percent copayment plan, for example, had 14 percent lower utilization, 19.9 percent fewer hospital admissions, and 25 percent less spending than the person whose care was free. These are surprisingly large figures, and they suggest that health care spending could be reduced significantly by the reintroduction of larger copayments. The Rand study may even understate the extent of savings possible from such a policy change: Study participants who drew plans with larger copayment requirements were compensated with income supplements, and many participants in the study reached their copayment limit quickly and thereafter care was free.

Extensive reliance on health insurance also fuels health care spending by contributing to some of the public health problems described in Chapter 3. Insurance spreads the cost of self-destructive conduct, such as drug and alcohol abuse, across a group of insureds, thereby lowering the cost to each individual. This increases the amount of activity being insured against, a phenomenon known as "moral hazard." A person with a drinking problem, for example, may worry about the effects his drinking will have on his health and marriage, but so long as he is insured he need not worry about medical bills caused by his condition. The impact of insurance on people's behavior can be indirect: Observation that the lifestyle-based ailments of friends and family members are routinely covered by insurance policies lulls us into discounting the long-term consequences of our own smoking, drinking, or overeating. Given the very large role that such conduct plays in driving health care costs in the U.S., even a small favorable effect on conduct would produce billions of dollars in savings.

Favorable tax treatment of employer-paid health insurance premiums, in a manner similar to that of government spending on health care, also has resulted in higher prices for other buyers of health services. The flow of patients with small copayments and wide coverage into the health care system once again makes it more difficult for the price-sensitive buyer to be heard. The value of the tax exemption for health insurance has been put at $48.5 billion a year.[12] These new dollars represent direct competition for the dollars of those consumers who are without employer-paid insurance. For them, the price of health care is higher because of overuse by insureds and overpayment by their third-party payers.

Beyond its effects on spending levels, current tax law raises serious questions of fairness. The law allows only persons with high medical expenses to claim a deduction against income taxes (though not Social Security taxes), and the Tax Reform Act of 1986 allows the self-employed and owners of unincorporated businesses to deduct from their taxable income only 25 percent of the premium cost of their own health insurance plans. Most persons who are unemployed or employees of small businesses that do not provide insurance get little tax relief. In effect, their cost of buying insurance is approximately twice as high as for those who receive employer-paid health insurance. The effective cost of buying a $4,000 policy for a family with an annual income of $35,000 is shown in Table 4-2.

Favorable tax treatment of employer-provided health insurance is unfair, too, because it delivers greater benefits to people with the highest taxable income. First, since the tax exclusion provides relief from payroll taxes, those in the highest tax brackets get the largest tax benefit. Second, there is no cap on the amount of insurance premiums that can be deducted from an employee's pre-tax income and claimed as a business expense, so the more lavish the insurance policy, once again the larger the tax benefit. Finally, those at the very low end of the pay ladder are below the minimum payroll tax threshold, and so they already do not pay income taxes.

There is reason to believe the nation's political leaders are becoming aware of the role that tax policy can play in the health insurance market. Effective January 1, 1991, a Refundable Health Insurance Tax Credit (RHITC) was made available to persons with at least one dependent child and adjusted gross income and earned income of less than $21,245. Families that buy health insurance that covers a child can receive a $426 credit.

In summary, we find that the tax exclusion for employer-paid health insurance has had a tremendous effect on health care spending as well as on access to care for people without such insurance. Favorable tax treatment has fueled a transition from individual responsibility for buying health care services and health insurance to extensive reliance on employer-paid insurance policies with low deductibles and copayment rates. This transition has meant greater demand for health care services, less monitoring of spending levels, and probably more health-damaging conduct. People with low incomes receive few or no tax benefits under the current arrangement and suffer doubly by having to pay higher prices for what insurance coverage they *are* able to afford.

If public policy reduced reliance on lavish employer-provided health insurance plans, billions of dollars could be saved as millions of consumers choose to purchase fewer health care services. Further savings would follow in the long term as more

Table 4-2. *Effective Cost of a $4,000 Health Insurance Policy for Family with Adjusted Gross Income of $35,000*

	100% Tax-Free Covered Policy[a]	25% Tax Deductible Self-Employed Policy[b]	100% Taxed Individually Purchased Policy[c]
Additional Earnings Needed to Purchase a $4,000 Health Insurance Policy	$3,716	$7,075	$8,214
Less 28% Marginal Federal Tax Rate	$ 0	-$1,701	-$2,300
Less 8% Marginal State Income Tax Rate	$ 0	-$ 486	-$ 657
Less Payroll Taxes	+$ 284	+$ 888	-$1,257
Policy Value	$4,000	$4,000	$4,000

[a] Funds used to purchase health insurance by an employer are exempt from federal, state, and local income taxes as well as Social Security taxes.

[b] Self-employed workers can deduct 25 percent of their health insurance costs from federal and state taxable income.

[c] Employees who purchase health insurance on their own must pay for their health insurance with after-tax dollars.

Source: Health Care Solutions for America, *Federal Tax Policy and the Uninsured*, January 1992, page 6.

health consumers became cost-conscious and better informed.

Government as Regulator

Health care buyers and sellers meet in a marketplace that is heavily influenced by government regulations. Regulations are imposed directly on the industry by each layer of government as well as indirectly by public policies influencing institutions outside the industry. Some of these laws were passed with the encouragement and support of the industry either to raise quality standards or limit competition. Others accompanied Medicare dollars but now have been extended well beyond the program to many parts of hospital administration and to the care provided to paying patients.

Six areas of regulation can be distinguished: regulations arising from the Medicare program, insurance mandates, supply restrictions, price controls, regulation of pharmaceuticals, and occupational licensing laws.

MEDICARE REGULATION. Many spokespersons for doctors and hospitals decry the burden of regulations arising from the Medicare program.[13] Implementation of DRGs was accompanied by new demands for recordkeeping, billing, and utilization reviews for privately insured patients as well as Medicare patients. Introduction in 1991 of Medicare's new physician reimbursement system—the Resource-Based Relative Value Scale (RBS)—is expected to make a bad situation worse. The *National Journal* has called RBS "the most sweeping regulatory scheme since the government imposed wage and price controls in the early 1970s."[14] The Washington D.C.-based Heritage Foundation calls RBS "the largest regulatory expansion in the history of the Medicare program" and "a regulatory nightmare."[15]

INSURANCE MANDATES. State governments have their biggest effect on health care costs by requiring insurance companies to cover specific treatments or therapies. The number of such mandates rose from 48 in 1974 to over 700 in 1991.[16] Common mandates are for treatment of alcoholism (49 states), chiropractic (37 states), podiatry (25 states), and drug addiction (25 states). According to John Goodman, president of the National Center for Policy Analysis, coverage for heart transplants is mandated in Georgia, liver transplants in Illinois, hair pieces in Minnesota, marriage counseling in California, pastoral counseling in Vermont, and deposits to a sperm bank in Massachusetts.[17] Goodman and economist Gerald Musgrave estimate that as many as 8.5 million people are priced out of the health insurance market by costly mandates.[18] Ending all state mandates could lower insurance costs by 30 percent.[19]

SUPPLY RESTRICTIONS. Most states enforce Certificate of Need (CON) programs requiring hospitals to receive state approval before making certain capital investments. The goal of the CON program was to encourage consolidation of small and presumably inefficient hospitals and to reduce duplication of services by hospitals. Empirical research has concluded that, while slowing growth in the number of hospital beds in a community, CON requirements either have increased or had no measurable effect on hospital expenditures.[20] This seemingly paradoxical finding is the result of two unintended consequences of CON programs: existing hopsitals use CON laws to prevent rivals, including lower-cost out-patient surgical clinics, from entering their markets; and hospital operating costs increase due to the failure to make more efficient investments in capital. In response to their poor performance, twelve states have eliminated CONs since 1983, and others are revising the way they are enforced. [21]

CON programs in combination with federal antitrust laws have put hospitals in a vise. On the one hand, CON programs admonish hospital administrators for over-investing in new facilities and encourage hospitals to cooperate in meeting their communities' health care needs more efficiently. On the other, federal antitrust laws have been rigorously applied to hospitals that "collude" or "conspire" with other hospitals to restrict competition. The U.S. Justice Department has prevented joint programs and mergers in recent years, costing hospitals millions of dollars in legal fees alone defending their plans in court.

PRICE CONTROLS. State governments routinely interfere in private-sector efforts to control health care spending. "Managed care," the label given to a variety of cost-containment programs based on insurer-provider agreements, now encompasses over half of all people with private insurance. Several states, however, interfere with the creation of managed care programs by fixing prices, limiting the range of prices that providers can offer, or limiting extra fees charged by insurers to enrollees who use providers who are not part of the agreement.[22] Access by insurers to the utilization records of their insureds has been limited in Maryland, and other states are considering similar restrictions.[23]

REGULATION OF PHARMACEUTICALS. The discovery and application of life-saving drugs is one of the brightest successes of the health care industry. The discovery of "miracle" drugs addressing tuberculosis, polio, coronary heart disease, and cerebrovascular disease have saved or improved over a million lives and saved $141 billion dollars in direct and indirect costs.[24] Despite these breakthroughs, spending on prescription drugs in the U.S. has fallen as a percentage of total health care spending from 7.4 percent in 1970 to 4.8 percent in 1990. (See Figure 4-4.) Per-capita spending on drugs in the U.S. is less than in Canada, Germany, and even Britain.[25]

Excessive regulation of drug manufacturers has reduced the cost savings and other benefits that drugs bring to the health care system. The Food and Drug Administration (FDA) is the government agency that attempts to ensure that drugs sold in the U.S. are safe and effective. Since there is always an element of risk involved in the introduction of any new drug, government regulators must (and do) balance the risk of harm posed by a new drug against the likely benefits it would bring. Because this balancing of costs and benefits is conducted in a political environment, however, regulators are biased toward rejecting applications for new drugs and making the approval process as time-consuming as possible. The reason, as University of Rochester political scientist David Leo Weimer has written, is that "the victims of adverse reactions are much more easily identified than those suffering because drugs beneficial to them have not been approved."[26] As a result, "beneficial as well as harmful drugs are precluded from the market."[27]

Figure 4-4. *Spending on Prescription Drugs as a Percent of Total Spending on Medical Care, 1970-1990*

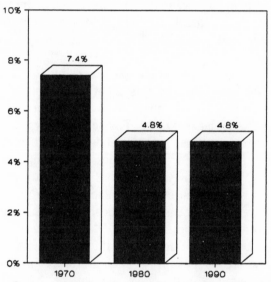

Source: Health Care Financing Administration, Office of the Actuary, 1993

Industry sources report that it now costs $350 million and can take as long as 12 years to bring a new drug to market.[28] The victims of overly lengthy and time-consuming testing processes for new drugs are largely invisible: They are the tens of thousands of people who die or suffer discomfort because the drug that *could* have helped them was not yet on the market. Only recently, with militant AIDS victims unwilling to wait the usual eight to ten years for a promising drug to finally reach the market, have the victims of bureaucratic delay been heard from.

A second way regulators interfere with an efficient market for life-saving drugs is by placing restrictions on the ability of physicians to choose the drugs they believe are best for their patients. These restrictions, often imposed on physicians by state governments in an attempt to slow the growth of state Medicaid spending, have no overall cost-saving effects and in some instances result in administrative expenses that exceed the cost of the drug prescriptions themselves.[29] A federal law passed in 1990 requires drug manufacturers to rebate a portion of their revenues back to state Medicaid programs as a condition for having their products listed in a national formulary. One industry source estimates that this indirect tax will cost the drug industry $6.4 billion between 1991 and 1995.[30]

OCCUPATIONAL LICENSING. Occupational licensing is a process by which state and local governments grant to groups of practitioners the power to forbid non-members from practicing particular skills or providing particular services. Physicians, physician assistants, registered nurses, practical nurses, and many other occupational groupings are licensed in most states. Licensing generally has come under heavy attack by economists and policy analysts as an expensive and sometimes counterproductive way to promote the public interest.[31] The licensing of health professionals also has been criticized by proponents of "alternative" health care modalities.[32] By restricting entry into the health profession, licensing laws restrict supply and therefore increase prices. Licensing discourages cost-saving innovations by codifying and requiring deference to existing knowledge. Licensing also interferes with the most efficient use of labor in a doctor's office or hospital by preventing nurses and trained personnel from performing tasks reserved for doctors.

State governments, most often responsible for regulating occupations, are often loath to repeal existing laws. There are, however, other, more politically acceptable, ways to expand the boundaries of health practices. One is "institutional licensing," which would grant a hospital, for example, greater leeway in defining the roles of the licensed and credentialed health professionals it employs. The hospital environment allows for closer monitoring of staffs and accountability for performance than do solo or small-group practices. If allowed to more broadly define the duties of registered nurses and licensed vocational nurses, for example, hospitals could economize on the time of physicians and specialists. The public would clearly benefit from this less costly provision of care.

In each of these ways, government unintentionally raises th'e cost of health care or health insurance. In the case of insurance mandates, the costs are in the billions. Over $200 billion was paid in private insurance premiums in 1990. If repealing coverage mandates could indeed reduce insurance costs by 30 percent, savings of $60 billion—nearly 10 percent of total health care spending in 1990—would be achieved.

These We Can Change

Government intervention has significantly and unnecessarily increased health care spending:

- The tremendous growth of government spending on health care during the 1970s and 1980s bid up prices and fueled a major expansion of the health care industry.

- Medicare and Medicaid expenditures were made in ways that encouraged excessive utilization and price inflation; more recently, these programs have caused cost shifting to privately insured patients.

- Federal and state tax policies encourage people to demand insurance policies with low deductibles and small copayment requirements, leading to price insensitivity, overuse of health services, and needless administrative expenses.

- Extensive regulation of the hospital industry, originally governing reimbursement for Medicare and Medicaid patients, now extends to care provided to all patients.

- State laws mandate insurance coverage for conditions ranging from alcoholism to hairpieces, costing health care consumers as much as $60 billion a year.

■ State and local laws limit competition among hospitals and restrict their investment decisions.

■ State regulations interfere with the creation and maintenance of PPOs and other insurer-provider agreements designed to control spending.

■ Over-regulation adds billions of dollars a year to the cost of developing and bringing to market new drugs, while delays caused by these requirements keep life-saving as well as cost-saving drugs off the market.

■ Occupational licensing laws increase salaries, discourage innovation, and perpetuate inefficient patterns of manpower utilization in doctor's offices and hospitals.

Spending on health care in the U.S. is too high because the prices of scarce medical resources are being bid up by tax-supported entitlement programs. Spending is too high because tax policies subsidize the purchase of health insurance, resulting in over-utilization and little concern for the prices paid by third-party payers. Spending is sent soaring even higher as state governments capitulate to special interest groups and legislate expensive mandates, regulations, and anti-competitive licensing laws.

There is an important difference between these factors responsible for unnecessarily high spending and those that explain high costs—the list presented at the end of Chapter 3. Value is produced when real needs are met. The cost factors identified in Chapter 3 represent, by and large, real needs for spending. We can work in many ways to reduce the need for health care, but until those needs are reduced the money spent addressing them is not wasted.

The spending factors identified in this chapter are different. They illustrate spending decisions that are not made by individual consumers weighing the costs and benefits of their decisions. Instead, they are made by government fiat—as in the case of insurance mandates and other regulations—or by consumers in the presence of government policies that distort the costs and benefits of spending decisions. These decisions lead to spending on goods and services that would not be valued so highly in a free and competitive marketplace. This spending accurately can be labeled wasteful.

In light of the fact that government is responsible for so much of the current inflation in health care spending, we ought to be skeptical of proposals that require even more government involvement. Alas, the current public policy debate is replete with such proposals.

CHAPTER FIVE

Non-Solutions

PERHAPS BECAUSE so many mistakes have been made, analysts know a great deal about what does *not* work in health care policy. Regrettably, policy makers in the U.S. seem doomed to repeat the mistakes. Most proposed "solutions" to the problem of high health care spending are actually non-solutions, reactions that have little relevance to the underlying causes of spending. The more grandiose the proposal, the less relevant it tends to be.

In this chapter we review four frequently advanced plans for reform: national health insurance, managed competition, mandatory employer-provided insurance ("play or pay"), and socialized medicine. Before doing so, we set the record straight on a focal point of the current debate: the problem of people without health insurance, the uninsured.

The Problem of the Uninsured

Approximately 37 million Americans, constituting 14.5 percent of the population of the U.S., were estimated to be without insurance at some time in 1991.[1] While considerable press attention has been devoted to the *number* of uninsured, less has been paid to who they are and why they are not insured. An investigation of these questions reveals that lack of insurance in most cases is a short-term phenomenon that only rarely is the result of being denied coverage. Moreover, the uninsured tend to be younger and healthier than the general public, and a surprisingly large number have incomes well above poverty.

LENGTH OF TIME WITHOUT INSURANCE. According to the U.S. Bureau of the Census, nearly one quarter of the U.S. population was without insurance for some period of time during the 28 months from February 1985 through May 1987.[2] However, only 4.3 percent of the population was without insurance for the entire period.[3] A study by the Urban Institute found that half of all uninsured lack insurance for four months or less, while only 15 percent are uninsured for more than 24 months. Seventy-six percent of all uninsured spells end within a 12-month period.[4]

Alarm over short-term uninsurance is unjustified for several reasons. A person in need of medical treatment who lacks insurance will not be turned away by health care providers. In fact, the National Health Interview Survey conducted in 1984 found that people who lack insurance make similar numbers of contacts with physicians and stay in hospitals similar lengths of time as people with insurance.[5] A 1990 study by Lewin-ICF estimated that the uninsured pre-Medicare population in the U.S. received $31.9 billion in health care services in 1988, a per-capita level of spending equal to about 60 percent of per-capita expenditures on the insured population.[6] If a patient has little money and is unable to borrow, he still will receive treatment at nonprofit and government hospitals. It is against the law for a nonprofit hospital to turn away a patient needing medical care; sanctions include revocation of tax-exempt status. (Fewer than 12 percent of hospitals in the U.S. are for-profit.) Patients who can afford to do so may pay for medical treatment out of pocket, from savings, or by borrowing money. Moreover, most health care needs are not emergency needs; hence, they can be postponed or scheduled to accommodate interruptions in insurance protection.

AGE AND INCOME OF THE UNINSURED. According to Henry Aaron of The Brookings Institution, 37.2 percent of those without insurance in the fourth quarter of 1988 were under the age of 25.[7] John Goodman estimates that two-thirds of the uninsured are under age 30, in age groups that have the lowest health care costs. "Because they tend to be young and healthy and have few assets to protect," writes Goodman, "they are likely to be very sensitive to the price of health insurance and to forego coverage voluntarily if the price is too high."[8]

Insurance at current prices is a bad deal for many young people: Generous, employer-provided policies often force younger members of the workforce to pay for the coverage of treatments much more likely to be used by older employees. Moreover, per-capita expenditures on health care for persons under 65 are much lower than for persons 65 and older.[9] Health insurance, by spreading the cost of health care across age cohorts, will over-charge younger buyers.

A sizable portion of the uninsured population is not poor. Forty percent of uninsured households have incomes of $20,000 or more; 22 percent have incomes of $30,000 or more; and 13 percent have incomes of $40,000 or more.[10] Many of these families could afford insurance if its price were not artificially inflated by some of the factors discussed in the previous chapter. Others can afford to buy insurance but simply choose not to.

REASONS FOR BEING UNINSURED. In a 1984 national survey, more than half of all people without health insurance said the primary reason for their lack of insurance is that they "cannot afford" it.[11] The second most common reason given was coverage by another plan, typically that of a parent or spouse. Fewer than one percent (0.8 percent) blamed poor health or age. Fewer people blamed restricted access to insurance due to the condition of their health than reported that they simply "do not believe in insurance" (1.0 percent).[12] (See Figure 5.1.)

According to the Employee Benefit Research Institute (EBRI), only 1 percent of the U.S. population under 65 is uninsurable.[13] Most people without insurance are young, healthy, and employed. For them, being uninsured is the result of the high cost of health insurance, *not* insurers' unwillingness to write policies.

Except for a very small part of the uninsured population, being uninsured is the result of the high cost of health insurance. Policy prescriptions, then, should focus on ways to make health insurance more affordable for people with low incomes and a more attractive investment for young and healthy people who can afford to buy insurance but choose not to.

One form of health insurance already exists that is affordable to many people who are currently uninsured, and is

Figure 5-1. *Primary Reason for Being Uninsured, National Health Interview Survey, 1984*

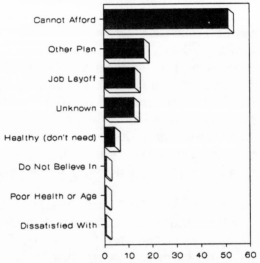

Source: Attiat Ott and Wayne Gray, The Massachusetts Health Plan: The Right Prescription? 1988

even a good deal for young and healthy persons. This insurance is catastrophic medical insurance, typically policies with annual deductibles of $3,000. Such policies cost just $125 per month in an average-cost city.[14] Premiums are so low because catastrophic insurance, unlike insurance with lower deductibles, is true *insurance* instead of pre-payment for routine medical expenses. Catastrophic insurance usually pays only for expenses that cannot be foreseen or influenced by the insured, but can be predicted by insurers for large groups of people.

The financial hardship that such high deductibles may pose on some families is a problem in need of solution. But it is important to understand that the availability of catastrophic insurance means the uninsured problem is different than what many reform advocates think. Most people can afford to buy insurance, but they cannot afford to set aside sufficient monies to *self-insure* for the large deductible that affordable insurance imposes on its buyers. If we could find a way to help people self-insure against routine medical expenses, we would solve the uninsured problem *and* the problem of insurance-driven price inflation in a single step. In fact, the authors propose just such a solution in the next chapter.

INSURANCE AND RISK. It is easy to forget, with insurance now so prevalent in the health care marketplace, that health insurance was rare before World War II and only reached its current high levels of coverage during the 1980s.[15] To be without insurance is risky, to be sure, but the evidence suggests that being without insurance for short periods of time does not result in poorer health or less access to health care. Why, then, are we surprised when some people choose to accept the risk and spend the money they save on other goods?

Some element of risk-taking is present in virtually everything we do. Twenty years ago the general public felt that individuals, not government, should weigh the risk of being uninsured against the benefits of spending money on other things. What has changed between then and now has less to do with health care costs than with public attitudes toward risk. As a nation we have become more risk-averse.[16] Calls for mandatory health insurance and national health insurance are calls to impose this new fear of risk on everyone.

Any worthwhile redesign of the U.S. health care system must expand access to care for those Americans now uninsured or under-insured, even if their numbers and needs may be less than some people claim. In the preceding chapter, we described how many government policies have unnecessarily lifted health care prices out of reach of persons who are low-income or unemployed. If, by repealing or changing these policies, we can significantly reduce the cost of health care and health insurance, then millions more Americans would find their access to quality health care restored. Moreover, the cost reductions brought about by effective reform would enable current government programs to better provide for those who truly cannot afford private health insurance.

National Health Insurance

A national health insurance plan would extend government health insurance to every citizen as a basic entitlement regardless of ability to pay. Such plans, sometimes referred to as "single payer" or "Canadian-style" programs, typically envision a single, government-administered system with deductibles, copayments, and coinsurance levels set very low or on a sliding scale based on income.[17] The plans would be funded by additional payroll taxes, savings generated by abolishing the tax exclusion for employer-provided health insurance, and such funds as currently are used to provide health care services to uninsured and indigent patients. The sale of private health insurance policies would be made illegal or limited to supplemental insurance for private rooms, prescription drugs, or services not covered by the government insurance program.

Proposals for national health insurance once dominated public debate over health care reform, and still are favorably reviewed by such organizations as the AFL-CIO and American Association of Retired Persons (AARP). Growing public awareness of the shortcomings of Canadian health care, together with President Clinton's decision to back a different reform strategy ("managed competition") have diminished the appeal of national health insurance plans. Still, variations on the single-payer model continue to circulate in state legislatures around the country.

IS IT NEEDED? The case for national health insurance rests on three assumptions: (1) The current system fails to provide adequate access to health care for a large number of people; (2) Health care costs would be reduced significantly by eliminating the costs associated with experience rating, insurance marketing and billing, and the different reimbursement methods used by different payers; (3) A single-payer system would give government greater leverage over physician fees and hospital investments in expensive technology and facilities, thereby making it possible to cap overall spending levels.[18]

The first assumption is unpersuasive in light of our earlier discussion. Medicaid, Medicare, state-run insurance pools, the new tax credit program for low-income families with children (described in the previous chapter), and charitable care provided by hospitals all act as safety nets for those who, for some reason, are unable to find insurance in the private market. If a problem remains in the insurance market, it is that health insurance prices are too high for many people who are unemployed or who work for companies that do not provide health insurance. The logical answer to this problem is to find ways to reduce the cost of insurance—repealing state mandates, for example, and extending favorable tax treatment to insurance premiums paid by individuals —not to abolish the private insurance system.

The second assumption, that costs would fall significantly under a single-payer system, is much disputed by analysts and representatives of the insurance industry.[19] Proponents of national health insurance believe that government programs should be more efficient than private programs because "publicly funded programs do not include costs for profits, marketing, or premium collection."[20] This is technically true, but it is also the reason estimates of the true costs of government programs so often are inaccurate. Profit-making is not allowed in the public sector, but this does not prevent its public-sector equivalent, "rent-seeking," from taking place.[21] As the discussion below of the Canadian national health insurance system demonstrates, rent-seeking has imposed tremendous costs on Canadian health care consumers.

Marketing and premium collection are activities that have their counterparts in government but often go by other names and are charged to the budgets of other government departments. Most importantly, these activities in the private sector can (but, unfortunately, under current conditions frequently do not) generate information that allows consumers to demand and providers to offer the options that best serve the needs of consumers.[22] This information is lacking in countries with national health insurance, leading many of them to adopt reforms aimed at generating such information.[23] If marketing by the health insurance industry does not now efficiently produce information about consumer preferences and provider capabilities, the solution (based on the discussion in Chapter 3) is to change tax policies, repeal state insurance mandates, and lift restrictions on negotiations among insurers, providers, and consumers. Abolishing the private insurance industry and replacing it with a government bureaucracy is unlikely either to lower spending or produce better information.

The third assumption on which the case for national health insurance rests is that such a program gives government greater ability to control health care spending. This is true, but is such control desirable? Government-imposed spending caps do not reduce health care *costs*, but merely health care *spending*. The true cost of a health care system is increased, not reduced, when government intervention causes waiting lines, slower recoveries, or larger numbers of preventable deaths. National health insurance allows government to set arbitrary limits on the number of dollars spent on health care. Whatever health needs are no longer met under such a cap do not disappear. They are merely shifted to health care consumers in the form of greater pain or pain of a longer duration, and sometimes earlier death.

WOULD IT WORK? There is no need to discuss national health insurance in theoretical terms only. Everyone, it seems, "knows" that Canada's national health insurance system is well-loved by its citizens, more fair than the U.S. system, and more successful in containing spending. State legislators across the country discuss "the Canadian model" as a point of departure for their own reform efforts. What does the Canadian experience tell us about national health insurance?

Canada's health care system is financed principally by taxes, while services are delivered primarily by physicians in private or group practice and nonprofit hospitals. Funding was once divided evenly between the federal government and the provinces, though that arrangement is changing. Payment for the system in the provinces of British Columbia, Quebec, and Ontario is based on a tax on individual payrolls. In the other provinces, a combination of sales and income taxes pays for the program.

Persons over 65 are not required to pay for the system, nor are individuals without income levels high enough to cover costs.

Private nonprofit hospitals are the norm in Canada, though their budgets are determined and investment decisions made by government. Projected utilization rates are negotiated between the province and local hospitals, and reimbursements are based on those rates. Patients may be charged premiums for special services such as private rooms, for which they are allowed to buy private supplemental insurance. Doctors are paid on a fee-for-services basis according to a schedule negotiated by the provincial government and the local medical society.

Although Canada has made a deliberate decision to control its health care spending, its record in this regard is dubious. While Canada has managed to keep its spending to approximately 8.5 percent of GDP, its high rate of economic growth relative to the U.S. obscures the fact that actual spending has risen quickly. Health policy analyst Edward Neuschler, examining per-capita spending by the U.S. and Canada between 1967 and 1987, found that "on an inflation-adjusted basis, the average growth rate over the 20-year period is slightly lower in the United States: 4.38 percent per year compared to 4.58 percent per year in Canada."[24] To ensure that his estimate had not obscured short-term trends in spending in the two nations, Neuschler also examined spending rates for five-year intervals between 1967 and 1987. The results, shown in Figure 5.2, reveal that per-capita health care spending in the U.S. grew at a slower rate than spending in Canada during three of the four periods.

That health care spending increases in Canada should have surpassed those in the U.S. during the 1970s and 1980s is remarkable for several reasons. The U.S. faced much more costly public health problems during the past 20 years than did Canada. For example, the U.S. teenage pregnancy rate in the 1980s was over twice as high as Canada's rate, and its incidence of AIDS three times as high.

Budget restrictions in Canada have led to the rationing of care and serious underinvestment in health technology and facilities. The waiting lists for health care in Canada have grown.[25] In British Columbia between November 1989 and

February 1990, the average wait for coronary artery bypass surgery was 23.7 weeks; for other open heart surgery, 21.4 weeks;

Figure 5-2. *Five-Year Average Growth Rates, Real Health Care Spending Per-Capita*

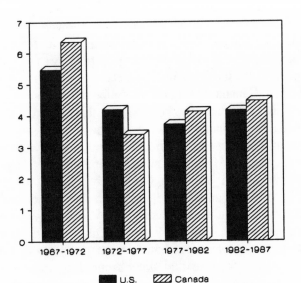

■ U.S.   ▨ Canada

Source. Edward Neuschler, "Canadian Health Care. The Implications of Public Health Insurance." 1990

for removal of varicose veins, 36.1 weeks; for cataract removal, 18.2 weeks; and for hernia repair, 24.6 weeks.[26] In the province of Newfoundland, the wait for a pap smear is up to five months —reduced to two months if the case is "urgent." The wait for a CAT scan is two months.[27] Canada does not allow patients to use private-sector treatment to avoid the waiting lists.

Press reports have suggested that individuals with sufficient wealth travel to the United States for medical services. In every province, the press reports the deaths of patients on waiting lists for coronary surgery.[28]

Canada trails far behind the U.S. in its investment in medical technology. The U.S. has three times as many CAT scanners per capita, 20 times as many pacemakers, and 60 percent more facilities for kidney patient treatment. According to the Vancouver-based Fraser Institute, the entire province of British Columbia has fewer CAT scanners than does the city of Seattle. There are fewer magnetic resonance imaging machines in all of Canada than in the state of Michigan.[29]

Hospital administrators in Canada have discovered that it is less costly to care for chronically ill patients—who primarily utilize the "hotel" services of a hospital rather than its surgical or specialty services—than to care for emergency patients. As a consequence, the portion of hospital beds in Canada occupied by terminally ill patients is higher than in the U.S., where such patients are placed in nursing homes. In Ontario, about 25 percent of all hospital beds are filled with chronically ill elderly.[30] The reason for this misallocation of scarce hospital beds is simple economics: Faced with government-imposed budgetary constraints and no opportunity to gain personally from treating more "expensive" patients, hospital administrators opt to turn away patients in need of acute care while attending to the boarding needs of the terminally ill.

Canada's efforts to control spending have resulted in deterioration of many hospitals and clinics. According to Edmund F. Haislmaier, an analyst for The Heritage Foundation, "Canada's hospitals have been living off their existing capital for twenty years, and more of them are gradually exhibiting the obsolescence and decay found in many British National Health Service hospitals."[31] Needed investments in facilities and equipment have been delayed in order to meet union demands and to supply more popular, labor-intensive health services.

While the Canadian health care system continues to enjoy favorable press coverage in the U.S., it is in fact undergoing significant change in Canada. In 1991, the Canadian federal government enacted a law capping federal funding of provincial health care systems.[32] Federal funding, which peaked in 1978/79 at 52.69 percent of total public-sector spending on health care in Canada, fell to just 37.47 percent in 1990/91.[33] It is widely expected that the provinces, unable to afford the programs in their current form, will move away from the single-payer model and adopt mixed public and private systems. The province of Ontario already is considering reorganizing its health system along the lines of a U.S. health maintenance organization (HMO), and over 65 percent of Canadians now purchase private supplemental insurance. Analysts predict that Canada will reintroduce private health insurance within the next five years.

What does all this say about the efficiency of national health insurance? Canada has imposed rationing and deliberately underinvests in technology and facilities, yet its rate of growth in per-capita spending is nearly the same as in the U.S. Canadians themselves are abandoning the single-payer model by phasing out federal support for it. The predicted cost savings of the single-payer model have not been realized in Canada, and there is little doubt but that quality of care has deteriorated as a result of the program. The overall efficiency of the Canadian health care system is almost certainly lower as a result of national health insurance.

COST ESTIMATES. If Canada remains a "model" despite its spending record, life-endangering queues, and underinvestment in necessary technology and facilities, one further hurdle remains to its adoption by the U.S.: its cost. Edward Neuschler puts the cost of adopting the Canadian Model in the U.S. market at between $244 and $252 billion in 1991 dollars.[34] Economists Aldona Robbins and Gary Robbins have placed the cost at $339 billion; they predict that implementing national health insurance would require a tax increase so large it would make "the United States one of the most heavily taxed among countries with whom we compete in international trade."[35]

A major reason why the U.S. cannot reduce its health care spending to the Canadian level is our reliance on physician specialists. Beyond their own higher incomes and training costs, specialists drive up costs by requiring more testing, performing more surgery, and demanding the newest technology. In the United States, fully 89 percent of all physicians are specialists; in Canada, just 60 percent are.[36] Indeed, the U.S. reliance on specialists stands out among all other countries in the world. The large number of specialists already working, combined with the number in the process of being trained, means it will be many years before a deliberate policy of reducing reliance on specialists would have any effect on the ratio of general practice physicians to specialists.

If national health insurance is adopted because of public expectations that it will save money, those expectations will either be sorely disappointed or met at the cost of dramatic reductions in the quality and quantity of health care services delivered. It should come as no surprise that popular estimates of the cost of these programs seriously underestimate their true costs: In recent years, government has shown itself singularly unable to appraise with any accuracy the cost of programs involving risk. Witness the banking and savings and loan bailouts, where cost estimates were increased two- and three-fold over the course of one year!

Managed Competition

Many people who once supported national health insurance have gravitated toward "managed competition," with the so-called Jackson Hole Initiatives being the most complete proposal to be advanced at the time of this writing.[37] Advocates of managed competition reject the single-payer model of a public-sector monopoly in health insurance, but contend that competition in the health care marketplace must be "managed" by government in order to correct "market failures."

WHAT IS MANAGED COMPETITION? The Jackson Hole Initiatives call for a "comprehensive reform of the economic incentives that drive the [health care] system."[38] Its authors contend that such action is necessary "to forestall massive public intervention into the U.S. health care system," presumably a reference to national health insurance or socialized medicine.[39] But it is difficult to describe the scale of intervention envisioned by the advocates of managed competition as anything less than "massive."

Under the Jackson Hole plan, insurers and providers would combine to form nonprofit, HMO-like organizations called Accountable Health Partnerships (AHPs). AHPs in turn would contract with large employers and huge purchasing agents called

Health Insurance Purchasing Cooperatives (HIPCs), each representing "at least several hundred thousand people."[40] The AHPs would be required to offer a menu of insurance programs to their members, with none of the plans offering less than a basic plan called Uniform Effective Health Benefits (UEHB) set by federal law.

The architects of the Jackson Hole plan anticipate that consumers and providers of health care will resist the new regime, so they propose regulations to compel participation. Care providers who do not join AHPs would not be allowed to bid for consumers represented by HIPCs, while those who *do* join would be exempted from the expensive state mandates described in Chapter Four. People whose employers refuse to join an HIPC would be denied the tax exemption for employer-paid insurance premiums. As our earlier analysis (also in Chapter Four) showed, managed competition thus would require these persons to pay a tax on insurance benefits consuming approximately half the value of their insurance. These employees would make up the difference from after-tax income or accept what insurance coverage is available at half the premium cost of their existing plans.

Once in place, the program would require more regulations to ensure that the participants compete fairly. An Outcomes Management Standards Board (OMSB), a Health Standards Board (HealSB), and a Health Insurance Standards Board (HISB) would be created, funded, staffed, and empowered to draft new regulations and standards affecting insurers and health care providers. A National Health Board (NHB) would act on the recommendations of the OMSB, HealSB, and HISB to determine the UEHB, certify AHPs and HIPCs, and oversee the entire program. The premiums on employer-provided insurance would be tax-free only up to the amount of the lowest-priced plan offered by the HIPC, forcing employers and employees to pay higher premiums for better plans with after-tax dollars. AHPs would be required to have annual open enrollment periods and accept all enrollees without medical reviews, waiting periods, or exclusion of coverage for pre-existing conditions. Should some AHPs attract groups with below-average risk levels, they would be required to transfer funds to AHPs that serve higher-risk groups.

The Jackson Hole Group believes that managed competition will "greatly reduce the cost and difficulty of taking further steps toward universal coverage."[41] These further steps include mandating that employers pay for insurance for all their full-time employees; requiring unemployed persons with income to pay a new tax equal to the price of the lowest-price plan offered by the HIPC responsible for their area; and requiring that persons enrolled in Medicare be allowed to receive care only from approved AHPs.

WHAT IS RIGHT ABOUT MANAGED COMPETITION? Proponents of managed competition are right to criticize the current open-ended tax exclusion for employer-paid health insurance benefits. There is a genuine need for employees who choose expensive benefit plans to bear the cost of that choice, and for changes in a tax policy that now rewards employees who choose to take compensation in the form of insurance rather than cash. These changes would dampen the demand for health care, reward providers who provide services most efficiently, and force inefficient providers to improve or leave the marketplace.

The Jackson Hole Group is also right to oppose proposals that would turn over complete responsibility for delivering health services to the government. Advocates of managed competition realize that "Government price controls simply do not work, especially in a field as complex and dynamic as health care. Regulators cannot manage utilization and appropriateness of care by remote control in an adversarial relationship with doctors."[42] Removing or changing public policies so that consumers and providers can discipline each other would make top-down regulation by government unnecessary.

The insight of managed competition advocates that large groups of insureds create economies of scale and a greater ability to spread risk than small groups is also on target. Bringing small employers together to jointly negotiate with insurers is a promising way to reduce administrative expenses, though *how this is done* while preserving choice and competition is problematic in the managed competition proposal. Private-sector success stories, such as a program operated by the Council of Smaller Enterprises

(COSE) in Cleveland, Ohio, could serve as a point of departure for further experiments and possibly regulatory reform.[43]

A final valuable recurring theme in managed competition literature is the need for more information on consumer choices and medical outcomes.[44] The typical health care consumer is ill-equipped to choose an insurer, doctor, or hospital because much of the information needed to make an informed decision is expensive to obtain or deliberately withheld by providers. Somehow, a more robust marketplace for information about health care choices needs to emerge.

"MARKET FAILURE" OR GOVERNMENT FAILURE? The Jackson Hole Group claims that the free market has failed to contain health care spending, price insurance fairly, and provide access to health care for everyone. It is because of this "market failure" that managed competition is needed.[45] But proponents of managed competition seem to be confusing "market failure" with "government failure," and this mistake leads them to an erroneous reform agenda.

Health care spending is high and rising for many reasons, many having little to do with how health care is financed. It is not "market failure" that fuels this part of demand for health services, but our rising wealth, aging population, unhealthy lifestyles, commitment to saving the very young and the very old, and other considerations raised in Chapter Three. By failing to recognize the dramatic role these factors play in explaining rising health care expenditures, managed competition advocates overstate the role our current finance and delivery systems play in causing rising spending levels.

Within the health care industry, unnecessarily high health care spending and restricted access to care typically are the results of failed government interventions. The growth of government spending on health care, rising ten-fold between 1970 and 1990, bid up the price of health care for all Americans. This was the result of government's failure to manage the growth of its new entitlement programs, not of the private sector's failure to meet new demand. Similarly, government's decision to exclude employer-paid insurance premiums from taxable compensation created excessive reliance on low-deductible, low-copayment insurance policies. This reliance, in turn, is why health care consumers appear to be so price-insensitive. In its role as regulator, government has caused higher drug prices, higher insurance premiums, and higher operating costs for hospitals.

Other than proposing to limit the tax exclusion for employer-paid health insurance, the Jackson Hole Group fails to support reforms that would remove the distortions and waste caused by past government failures. The proponents of managed competition behave like the man who, deciding he no longer liked the furniture he owned, bought additional furniture and crowded it into his house alongside the old furniture. His home now looked worse instead of better, and he could hardly walk from one room to the next! Instead of adding good furniture to bad, he should have removed the offending furniture as the new furniture was being acquired. So too should health care reformers consider removing *existing* policies that now distort incentives and cause unnecessary spending before proposing new interventions.

IS MANAGED CARE SO GOOD? The Jackson Hole Initiatives would virtually require that all doctors and consumers join Health Maintenance Organizations (HMOs)—a system of care delivery in which doctors are paid a salary or annual per-patient fee and patients are not allowed to see doctors who are not a part of the HMO.[46] According to managed competition proponents, this would be beneficial because HMOs are more efficient than fee-for-service provision, make continuous assessment of quality and productivity possible, and can accommodate such "equity-enhancing" policies as community rating (whereby everyone in a geographic area is charged the same price for insurance regardless of health) and automatic coverage for pre-existing conditions.

This rush to impose one style of health care delivery on all doctors and consumers seems ill-advised. Enrollment in Preferred Provider Organizations (PPOs), which allow greater patient choice, was more than twice that of HMOs in 1991.[47] The number of employers offering HMOs to their employees has not grown since 1987, and the percentage of employees who choose HMOs when offered the choice has stayed at approximately 33 percent since 1988.[48] Those HMOs that most closely resemble the Jackson Hole

Group's model, called staff and group HMOs, are experiencing the slowest enrollment growths, rising at an average annual rate of less than 6 percent between 1980 and 1990.[49]

HMOs have the potential to reduce health care spending, but many HMOs fail to realize this potential. Half of the employers responding to a recent survey by A. Foster Higgins, an employee benefits consulting firm, said their HMO rates were as high or higher than their non-managed care plan costs.[50] On average, the survey found that HMOs save employers 14.7 percent against traditional fee-for-service plans, but "many individual HMOs, PPOs, and point of service plans do not. Survey results show substantial variations in cost savings by geographic region. In some cities the average cost per employee for HMO coverage is actually higher than the average per employee cost for indemnity plan coverage."[51] A Congressional Budget Office survey of research found that enrolling Medicare patients in HMOs "had little or no effect on hospital use and costs."[52]

As mixed as the cost-saving record of HMOs has been, the record of managed care generally has been worse. "Some very basic questions about managed care remain unanswered," write Robert Miller and Harold Luft in a 1991 *Health Affairs* article. "We do not even know if managed care saves money."[53] Although individual employers report some savings with HMOs and PPOs, it is unknown whether their savings are simply offset by higher prices charged to patients not covered by managed care agreements. The Congressional Budget Office survey cited earlier concluded that "During the past decade, managed care appears to have had little effect on total health care spending in the nation."[54] In 1993, the Congressional Budget Office went further and said a national managed competition program would cost $270 billion over five years before it could be expected to save money, and even then savings would be very doubtful.[55]

Not only are the cost savings attributed to HMOs elusive, but the fairness of their community rating strategy is also questionable. By not allowing insurance premiums to reflect risk, community rating forces low-risk persons to subsidize high-risk persons. In practice, young families with relatively low incomes will be subsidizing the health care of older and financially better-off families. Families headed by a parent aged 19 to 24 have less than half the income and one-third the medical expenses of the typical family headed by a parent aged 55 to 64.[56] Under community rating, both families would pay the same insurance premiums. Is this fair?

Community rating poses other problems. It subsidizes behavior that leads to higher health care costs, the "moral hazard" problem discussed in Chapter 4. This in turn raises health care costs for everyone, hurting particularly the uninunsured. When employers offer community-rated HMOs *and* risk-underwritten fee-for-sevice plans, healthy people tend to enroll in the HMOs, forcing the insurers of the fee-for-service plans to raise rates.[57] HMOs may deliberately encourage this biased selection pattern by offering more services that appeal to younger, healthier enrollees. Conventional fee-for-service plans attempt to control rate increases by raising deductibles and copayments. The end of this complex process of shifts and adjustments may be the delivery of too many services to healthy HMO enrollees and too little coverage for high-risk enrollees in conventional fee-for-service plans.

(As this book goes to press, we understand that the Jackson Hole Initiatives are being revised to require that the Health Insurance Purchasing Cooperatives offer at least one open-ended Accountable Health Partnership, which would allow consumers the option of going to any provider. While this change reflects the public's desire to retain the right to choose physicians, it nevertheless would perpetuate the process of biased selection that leaves high-risk persons less well-off.)

Finally, the attempt by managed competition proponents to put HMO-like organizations into place across the country simply is not *feasible* in the United States. HMOs depend heavily on primary care physicians: They are the salaried professionals who staff HMOs, acting as "gatekeepers" to direct their patients' use of all health care services. To establish HMOs nationwide, then, would require many more primary care physicians than are now in the system. As noted earlier in this discussion, there literally are not enough primary care physicians in the United States to perform the gatekeeper function. To apply the HMO solution nationally in the form of "managed competition" would require a supply of general practitioners that simply does not exist and *will not* exist for ten or fifteen years.

CAN REGULATION CREATE THE RIGHT INCENTIVES? The Jackson Hole Group believes that regulations handed down by a new government bureaucracy are necessary to create a new system of economic incentives for the health care industry. But this is a strange kind of logic since *regulation itself* is usually at fault for creating a divergence between individual self-interest and the broader interests of society. Lawful actions in a regulated environment often do not create social value, but instead involve "working the system" to transfer wealth and power from one group to another. The Jackson Hole Initiatives, unfortunately, appear likely to produce incentives to engage in this kind of unproductive conduct.

The National Health Board, says the Jackson Hole Group, would be "an independent, quasi non-governmental agency"[58] that would make its decisions "on the basis of science and values, not politics."[59] But many prominent economists and political scientists believe that such a government agency is impossible in theory and has never existed in fact.[60] Government agencies by their very nature are subject to political pressures and inevitably make their decisions based on political considerations. Decisions made by the NHB would produce concentrated benefits for some interest groups and big losses for others. Both winners and losers would try to influence the agency's decisions. Because they are more easily organized and more motivated than the general public, they would succeed in getting laws passed that may not be in the general public's interest.[61]

In practice, government agencies created to make policies "on the basis of science and values" routinely are captured by the very industries they were created to regulate. This story has been told of the oil industry,[62] electric and other utilities,[63] airlines,[64] zoning commissions,[65] and many others. Even Alain Enthoven, a chief advocate of managed competition, acknowledges that "Regulators become 'captured by the regulated.'"[66] If this occurs to the NHB, who can doubt that its powers will be used to advance the special interests of some groups of providers and consumers at the expense of others? Creation of this arbitrary power moves us further away from a system where private incentives support the public good.

Past attempts to use regulation to achieve cost savings and other desirable effects in the health care industry have produced poor results. Insurance mandates have been used by small interest groups to require that everyone who buys insurance must help pay for their hair transplants, artificial insemination, and other medical procedures of questionable public value. Certificate of Need programs have been used by hospitals to restrict competition and block construction of cost-saving out-patient medical clinics. The introduction of Diagnosis Related Groups (DRGs) and most recently the Resource-Based Relative Value Scale (RBS) have added tremendously to the administrative costs of hospitals.

The record of regulation in industries outside of medicine is equally poor. William A. Niskanen of the Cato Institute estimates that complying with federal regulations alone cost $400 billion in 1990, roughly $4,000 per household.[67] Thomas Hopkins of Rochester Institute of Technology puts the cost at $392 billion per year.[68] The high cost and unsatisfactory results of regulation helped spur a long list of deregulation efforts in the U.S. extending to trucking, airlines, long-distance phone service, railroads, buses, oil, and natural gas. "The verdict of a great majority of economists," wrote Alfred Kahn in 1989, "would, I believe, be that deregulation was a success."[69]

Why, in the light of the dismal record of past regulatory efforts, do advocates of managed competition believe *more* regulation would deliver lower costs and higher quality? And why, when *de*regulation is being applied and working in many other industries, do they propose turning back the clock in the health care industry?

CONCLUSION. Managed competition is not the solution to our nation's health care problems. To a large extent, the Jackson Hole Group has misdiagnosed the problem: It is not "market failure" that causes high spending and limited access to care, but "government failure." Their proposed solution, an HMO-style organization on a national scale, requires more primary care physicians than we now have or can train before the end of the century. Nor would such a program bring about the changes in incentives that its advocates write about. Instead, we will see an expansion of regulatory and bureaucratic excess, problems that already plague the health care industry. Instead of empowering consumers so they can demand better service at lower prices, managed competition replaces what little power consumers now have with an arbitrary power placed in the hands of a new government bureaucracy.

The Jackson Hole Group's criticism of the traditional fee-for-service relationship between doctors and patients misses the mark. The vast majority of goods and services in the U.S. are purchased on a fee-for-service basis, yet we do not worry that this encourages restaurant owners to serve us too much food, for example, or auto mechanics to sell us too many tires. We trust that consumers, looking out for their own best interests, will counter the natural desire of providers to sell as much as possible at as high a price as possible.

Regrettably, regulation and excessive reliance on insurance have made health care consumers passive and undemanding, willing to be over-served and over-charged because a third party pays the bill and regulations often limit competition among providers. The solution is not to abolish fee-for-service medicine or the conventional risk-underwritten insurance that funds it. It is instead to genuinely change the incentives of consumers and providers by changing tax policy, repealing regulations, and restoring true consumer sovereignty in the health care marketplace. Reforms that would accomplish these objectives are described in the next chapter.

Mandatory Employer-Provided Insurance

A third "non-solution" to the problem of high health care costs is to mandate that employers provide insurance coverage to all their full-time employees. The logic of such a proposal is as follows. A sizable portion of the uninsured population works for employers that do not provide insurance.[70] The many businesses that *do* provide insurance coverage for their employees are at a competitive disadvantage vis-a-vis those that do not. Requiring that all businesses provide insurance thus would "level the playing field," extend insurance coverage to many who now lack it, and avoid new taxes or increased government spending.

In order to compel businesses to offer their employees insurance, most plans for mandatory employer-provided insurance have a "play or pay" provision whereby an employer may choose to pay a payroll tax of some amount (typically 7 to 9 percent) instead of purchasing insurance.[71] Revenue from the payroll tax would fund a public health insurance program for those not covered by private insurance.

Mandatory employer-provided insurance would seem to have important advantages over other methods of expanding health care coverage, particularly when the alternative involves even greater government intervention into the health care marketplace. These benefits include lower costs of administration (by utilizing the private insurance market for enrollment and claims processing); avoiding unnecessary duplication of facilities (by utilizing existing capacity in private hospitals); and better utilization of existing health care facilities (by bringing currently uninsured people into managed care programs).

But a play or pay program also would have disadvantages. These disadvantages are its adverse effect on small businesses and the working poor, the likelihood that many private employers would choose to drop existing insurance policies in favor of the less-expensive public program, and the likelihood that the public insurance program would grow uncontrollably in size and cost, giving us the worst elements of national health insurance without any of its (however unlikely) benefits.

EFFECT ON WORKING POOR. In a recent editorial on "play or pay," *The New York Times* said "The lowest-paid workers would be hardest hit."[72] *The Washington Post* agreed, saying "Among the great unspoken disadvantages of this is that it would likely be regressive, hurting the very people it is meant to help, in that left to itself the increased cost would further depress the wages of the already low-paid workers who are the majority of the working uninsured."[73] Why would play or pay, which is intended to benefit the working poor, have just the opposite effect?

Play or pay puts the burden of insurance on employers. Large companies and companies that employ high-paid workers might be able to raise prices to recover the cost of the new benefit or reduce salaries by the amount of the new burden. But small businesses and businesses that pay low wages often are unable to make these adjustments, and must instead lay off employees. If salaries are already at or near the minimum wage, for example, making an offsetting wage reduction would be illegal. The Institute for Research on the Economics of Taxation (IRET) explained how play or pay would affect small businesses like this:

> The burden of any payroll tax is borne by both the employer and the employee. While the employer pays the tax directly, the employee pays his or her share through reduced wages or wage increases. For those working at or near the minimum wage, any reduction in wages is not an option. To the extent that these workers do not have a productivity rate that would justify the . . . proposed increase in the cost of keeping them employed, their jobs will be eliminated. This also suggests that new jobs for lower skilled workers would ultimately be created at a much slower rate.[74]

Rather than cut salaries, many employers would lay off workers or slow down the expansion of their workforces. The Partnership on Health Care and Employment estimates that between 630,000 and 3.5 million workers would lose their jobs under a mandatory insurance plan.[75] The National Center for Policy Analysis puts the job loss at 1.1 million, and estimates a reduction in GNP of $27 billion and an increase in the federal deficit of $46.5 billion.[76] By making it likely that low-paying and entry-level jobs would be eliminated, mandatory employer-provided health insurance would increase the number of persons unable to purchase insurance or pay medical expenses directly.

PAYING RATHER THAN PLAYING. If set at 7 or even 9 percent, the payroll tax proposed in play-or-pay plans would be considerably less than what most small businesses now pay for insurance. The average employee's health benefits now cost an employer over $3,000 per year. The cost of buying insurance for a worker making $20,000 a year, therefore, is 15 percent of payroll, as much as twice the cost of paying the new payroll tax. Adding a $3,000 insurance plan to the salary of a $10,000/year worker represents a 30 percent increase in compensation, more than four times the cost of the tax. Obviously, many employers will be tempted to "pay" rather than "play."

Setting the payroll tax too low will lead many employers to "dump" their employees into the public insurance plan. A study of play or pay conducted by the Urban Institute for the U.S. Department of Labor estimates that play or pay would result in 42.5 million people losing their employer-sponsored plans and being forced to enroll in the public insurance program.[77] According to the study, more non-elderly Americans would be enrolled in the public program than would be left in the private insurance sector. The study prompted then-Labor Secretary Lynn Martin to say play or pay "is backdoor national health insurance."[78]

According to John Goodman, "in the vast majority of their cases employers will have strong incentives to pay the tax rather than begin providing coverage themselves. . . . Nor is this mere speculation. An aide to Sen. Edward Kennedy says the bill's sponsors expect this to happen."[79] The 7 percent payroll tax rate bears no relationship to the actual cost of insurance; it is *intended* to create a single, tax-subsidized and government-operated insurance system by driving private insurers out of the market. Consequently, many of the reservations expressed regarding national health insurance apply with equal force to play or pay.

MORE PRICE INFLATION. Under play or pay, the cost of insurance is likely to increase even faster than in the past. Since health insurance no longer would be subject to contract negotiations between management and labor, employers and employees no longer would be able to weigh the benefits of insurance against its costs. Since purchase of the policy would be mandatory, premiums could be expected to rise, and complex formulas and regulatory mechanisms to determine the "just" price undoubtedly would find their way onto next year's legislative agenda.

Pressure could be expected to mount for expanding the range of treatments covered by the mandated insurance policies, just as state insurance mandates have multiplied in recent years. Experience tells us that Congress would be even less able than state legislatures to resist calls from special interest groups to widen the range of benefits contained in the "basic" mandated policy. The result would be rising insurance premiums and still more employers dropping their private insurance coverage and choosing instead to pay the payroll tax.

As companies with poor health-claims experience turn over their workforces to the tax-funded public program, its costs would rise disproportionately. Alain Enthoven predicts the following results:

> Those most likely to choose the government insurance plan would be those with the lowest pay and the highest medical costs. So revenues would fall short, and costs would run over global budgets. If the government raised the payroll tax to compensate for these increased costs, the relatively healthy and better paid would be motivated to leave the public program. The likely outcome would be to limit the tax, under pressure from small business, and to add to the federal deficit. The scenario would be a replay of the fiscal disasters we are observing in the Federal Savings and Loan Insurance Corporation, the Federal Deposit Insurance Corporation, and Medicare Hospital Insurance.[80]

The discussion in this section can be summarized quickly. Mandating employer-provided health insurance is hardly a "free" way to extend insurance to the working uninsured. Plans under consideration now in Washington would destroy as many as 3.5 million jobs and reduce GNP by as much as $27 billion. Mandatory health insurance would cause insurance rates and health care spending to spiral upward over time as captive participants spend less time and money monitoring the programs and as special interest groups succeed in adding expensive coverage mandates. Mandatory insurance would cause many employers to "dump" at first their less healthy employees, and then all employees, into the public insurance program, thereby gradually destroying the private insurance market and fueling further health care price inflation.

The failure of play or pay can be traced to the fact that it does not address the causes of unnecessarily high health care costs. Since it is *affordability*, not availability, that is the primary cause of the problem of the uninsured, mandated insurance is a short-term response that makes the longer-term problem worse.

Socialized Medicine

Socialized medicine is distinct from national health insurance. While the latter would shift *funding* responsibility to the public sector, the former would shift into the public sector both the funding and the *delivery* of health care.

The phrase "socialized medicine" is in disrepute among policy analysts and health care experts, perhaps for good reason. The late Albert W. Snoke, formerly of Yale University, expressed the prevailing mood well when he wrote, "I find it difficult to understand what is meant when an individual or organization criticizes a medical or health program as 'socialized medicine.' The definitions of this term are usually fuzzy or self-serving. Too frequently it seems as if 'socialized medicine' means any change from the existing system, especially if it is a program with which the doctor or organization disagrees."[81]

The authors of the present discourse have a more precise definition in mind. We refer to plans whereby ownership of the "factors of production" of health care is largely or entirely in government hands. By this definition, the United States does not have socialized medicine: Government spending may account for some 42 percent of total health care expenditures, but only 1,843 of the nation's 6,780 hospitals (27.2 percent) are government-owned. Canada also does not have socialized medicine since most care is delivered by private, albeit heavily regulated, hospitals. Two nations that clearly *do* have socialized medicine are Britain and the Soviet Union (now the Confederation of Independent States). Significantly, both are in the process of dismantling their systems.

Why even discuss socialized medicine today? Although proposals for socialized medicine no longer seem to be a significant part of the public policy debate in the U.S., it is important that the record of socialized medicine be documented and understood. *Some sixty years ago, it was popular to point to the Soviet health care system as a model of efficient organization and universal access to care.*[82] As it became apparent that this system presented severe quality and equity problems, advocates of socialized medicine abandoned the Soviet example and embraced the British system.[83] During the past ten years, popular awareness of the deterioration of the British health care system has led to the abandonment of this example as well. Today, most advocates of socialized medicine favor national health insurance as a way to achieve many of the goals once thought to be best attained by socialism.

The proponents of national health insurance should not be allowed to walk away from failed efforts to implement their ideas. These failures need to be explained. If the explanation reveals problems that are inherent in government funding or ownership of health care facilities, then proponents of these ideas today must show why they will not also fail.

From an economic perspective, the difference between national health insurance and socialized medicine is one of degree, not kind. In Canada, for example, government determines the fees that doctors may charge, approves hospital budgets, pays most health care expenses, and forbids private insurers from competing with the national system. That doctors and hospital administrators are not direct employees of the state, and hospitals hold charters indicating that they are private and nonprofit, does not change the fact that doctors and hospital administrators in Canada act in many ways as if they were government employees.

As the following discussion of Britain's health care system will document, Canadian and British patients and health care providers face many of the same perverse incentives and typically respond in similar ways. That the Canadian system is "pluralistic" while the British system is "socialized" may be an important distinction to maintain in some contexts. But we should not allow this distinction to obscure the fact that the maladies of socialized medicine are often the same as those afflicting or about to afflict national health insurance systems.

SOCIALIZED MEDICINE IN BRITAIN. Britain's "cradle-to-grave" National Health Service (NHS) was created in 1948 with the vision of providing all needed services equally to the entire population. Britons are granted access to basic medical services at little or no direct cost to them as patients; nearly the entire cost is socialized through taxes. Nominal fees for prescriptions are charged to the wealthy. General tax revenues and a minor payroll deduction provide revenue for the system. The NHS owns and operates over 2,000 hospitals and employs the staff. Doctors also are employed by the NHS, but they are allowed to maintain private practices as well. Approximately 10 percent of health care spending in Britain is financed through the private sector.

Attempts by the British government to control health care costs have taken the form of limiting access to services that Americans take for granted. In Britain, the waiting list for surgery is near 800,000 out of a population of 55 million.[84] Purchases of state-of-the-art equipment have not been made. In Britain, few CAT scanners are available in the National Health Service; ironically, the British invented the device and export almost half of the CATs used in the world. One of the developers of kidney dialysis was British, and yet the country has one of the lowest dialysis rates in Europe.

The Brookings Institution has estimated the number of British patients denied access to treatment annually. Its analysts found that 7,000 Britons in need of hip replacement, between 4,000 and 17,000 patients in need of coronary bypass surgery, and some 10,000 to 15,000 patients in need of cancer chemotherapy are denied medical attention in Britain each year. Table 5-1 shows the number of patients denied five types of treatment in Britain along with the estimated additional costs of providing service to those patients.

In Britain, the elderly have borne the brunt of government-imposed spending ceilings. Age discrimination is particularly

Table 5-1. *Rationing Care in the British National Health Service*

	Number of Patients Denied Treatment Each Year	Added Cost of Treating These Patients (millions)
Renal Dialysis	9,000	$140
Cancer Chemotherapy	10,000-15,000	40
Total Parenteral Nutrition	450-1,000	45
Coronary Artery Surgery	4,000-17,000	175
Hip Replacement	7,000	50

Source: Calculations by John Goodman based on Henry J. Aaron and William B. Schwartz, *The Painful Prescription: Rationing Hospital Care* (Washington, DC: The Brookings Institution, 1984).

apparent in the treatment of chronic kidney failure. Britain's Office of Health Economics reported in 1980 that 55-year-old patients were refused treatment at 35 percent of dialysis centers; at age 65, 45 percent of the centers refused treatment; patients 75 or older rarely received treatment.[85]

In addition to estimates of treatment denial, a measure of the accessibility of health care is the degree to which medical technology is available. Table 5-2 shows the availability of three life-saving inventions in eight developed countries, including Britain. All three—pacemakers, CAT scanners, and renal dialysis —are commonly available in the United States. In each of the three cases, availability in the U.S. exceeds that in the other seven nations. CAT scanners are six times more available in the U.S. than in Britain. Similarly, pacemakers are used here at four times the rate of Britain, and kidney patient treatment in the United States was 60 percent greater than in Britain.

As is the case in Canada, hospital administrators in Britain have discovered that it pays to turn away patients needing surgery and other specialized services while catering to the terminally ill.

Table 5-2. *Availability of Modern Technology in the 1970s*

	Pacemakers per 100,000 Population 1976	CAT Scanners per million Population 1979	Kidney Dialysis and/or Transplants per million Population 1976
Australia	7.3	1.9	65.8
Canada	2.3	1.7	73.4
France	22.6	0.6	111.3
Italy	18.8	NA	102.0
Japan	2.7	4.6	NA
United Kingdom	9.8	1.0	71.2
United States	44.2	5.7	120.0
West Germany	34.6	2.6	105.0

Source: National Center for Policy Analysis.

One in four hospital beds in Britain is occupied by a terminally ill patient, resulting in reduced access to care for large numbers of Britons.

   To summarize, socialized medicine has had a strong negative impact on the quality of health care in Britain. It has led to less investment in life-saving technology; rationing of essential health care services; and featherbedding of such proportions as to severely restrict access to hospital beds by persons in desperate need. Rather than promote wider public access to quality health care, the British system appears to have exacerbated inequity by encouraging discrimination based on age and type of service needed.

   British consumers, like their Canadian counterparts, have responded to the low quality of care by encouraging a growing private market in health care. The number of people holding private insurance coverage in Britain has doubled in the last ten years and now approaches 12 percent of the population.[86] In January 1989, the British government published a white paper calling for a major shift in the NHS toward competition and choice. District Health Authorities, once monopoly suppliers of services to the people in their districts, are now purchasers of services from public as well as private providers, including those outside their territory. Britain's experiment with socialized medicine, it appears, is almost over.

SOCIALIZED MEDICINE IN THE SOVIET UNION. Until its recent devolution into apparently independent states, the Soviet Union boasted the world's largest and oldest socialized health care system. By all objective accounts, it has been a disaster. Studies conducted in the 1970s indicated that one-third of all cases of illness in cities, and two-thirds of illnesses in rural areas, were not treated by doctors.[87] During the 1980s, significant upward trends in the prevalence of typhoid, diphtheria, whooping cough, measles, mumps, hepatitis, and salmonellosis were reported.[88] Incredibly, the crude mortality rate in the Soviet Union rose from 7.1 to 10.8 deaths per 1,000 between 1965 and 1984, a peacetime increase previously unknown in recorded history.

Despite its public claims to the contrary,[89] access to care in the Soviet health system was deliberately non-egalitarian. Special "closed" systems provided health care for favored citizens affiliated with the communist party or other political institutions. Care in these systems was better-funded than in facilities open to the general public, though still far below the standards set in other countries. Queuing for health services, common to all socialized health care systems, has been called "pervasive" and "systemic" in the Soviet Union.[90] Queues formed for first contacts with physicians, for basic diagnostic procedures, and for virtually all forms of surgery. Bribery was a common way to move ahead in a queue, to get clean sheets, or even to be served edible food.

Just how bad are conditions in Soviet hospitals today? According to a Soviet newspaper account in June 1991, conditions were so bad that women "run away by climbing out of windows" rather than stay for the required two to three days after abortions are performed. According to the newspaper, "there is no medicine, no equipment, no qualified or conscientious personnel," and as a result, "the last of the specialists are already sitting on their suitcases" waiting to emigrate.[91]

WHY SOCIALISM FAILS. It is well documented that costs in the public sector are routinely higher than in the private sector, the result of rent-seeking by various interest groups within the public sector in the absence of marketplace discipline.[92] Over time, investment decisions made by a political process diverge from those that are most efficient, leading to such commonly observed public-sector maladies as control by powerful unions, deferred maintenance, reliance on outdated technologies, and extremely short planning horizons. Such problems have been observed in the Canadian and British national health care systems as well as other socialized health care systems around the world.

As noted earlier, profit-making, marketing, and transaction costs all exist in the public sector as well as in the private sector. In the public sector, administrators and elected officials use their positions to acquire power, prestige, perks, and higher salaries for themselves. Experience has shown that this "rent-seeking" often leads to poor stewardship over public funds and efficiency losses that exceed whatever profits a private firm might have made delivering the same service.

Public ownership of schools,[93] mass transit systems,[94] and the U.S. Postal Service[95] has created a record of mismanagement and underinvestment that has been carefully studied and documented. In each case, investments in technology and facilities are postponed to pay off politically influential public-sector labor unions. The monopoly position that often comes with public ownership of an enterprise dramatically strengthens the ability of labor to use its threat of strike action during wage negotiations, since strikes would completely close down a city's schools, public transit, or mail delivery. In each instance where public ownership has become the rule in the U.S., public-sector wages have risen well above private-sector levels, while productivity and output have fallen well below comparable levels. There is little reason to expect that the experience would be different in the field of health care, and indeed, the experience of other countries conforms to our expectations.

Private markets work because they allow individuals to evaluate their options and take responsibility for their choices. Since the value anyone places on a particular good or service is subjective, we cannot "second guess" consumers by making decisions for them. The failure of socialism is largely the story of government's failed attempts to make consumption and investment decisions for individuals.

It is sometimes asserted, as an argument for socialized medicine, that health care is "different": because the average consumer lacks the knowledge to correctly evaluate options, because health care is such an important service, or because a person's contact with a health care provider often occurs in an emergency life-threatening situation.[96] These arguments all ring hollow.[97] Is the average consumer sufficiently knowledgeable about nutrition to buy his own meals, or about automobiles to choose a safe vehicle? Are food or transportation any less "important" than health care? Why should we allow freedom of choice and competition among providers in these fields but not in the health profession? Are health care providers any less honest or reliable than grocers or auto dealers? And only a very small percentage of health care decisions take place in emergency rooms; the vast majority are made in non-emergency situations with ample time for consultation.

Socialism doesn't work well to organize supply and demand generally, and the record shows that it has been an especially harmful failure in providing health care. Perhaps government is so unable to provide health care services efficiently because the value we each place on health is so personal, so *subjective*.[98] Choice and personal responsibility for choosing seem the only way to price health care accurately.

Conclusion

The rising cost of health care and health insurance has contributed to an increase in the number of people without health insurance. While public policy makers are correct to take notice of this trend, a review of the evidence suggests that the situation is less dire than we have been led to believe. The great majority of cases of uninsurance are for short periods of time; people without insurance tend to be younger and healthier than the general public; and lack of insurance in most cases does not arise from personal health problems or result in reduced access to health care. Rather than abolish the private health insurance system, a smarter prescription would be to change public policy to help the 1 percent of the under-65 population that is genuinely uninsurable and reduce the cost of insurance for the many millions of people who now cannot afford it.

National health insurance, now being promoted as a solution to both the nation's rising health care spending and to the problem of the uninsured, is not likely to solve either. Canada has not seen the cost-containment promised by advocates of national health insurance. It has, however, seen a variety of consequences that have reduced the quality of health care received by Canadians. These consequences—longer queues, underinvestment in technology, and deterioration of facilities—can be expected to accompany any move to national health insurance in the U.S.

Managed competition, another proposed solution, is also flawed. Its model—the HMO that accepts all applicants while controlling costs—has not worked as well as advertised. Managed competition would require government interventions nearly as large and expensive as those envisioned by advocates of national health insurance. Patient choice of physicians and control over the process would be limited as an array of new and impersonal "quasi non-governmental" bureaucracies arise to enforce compliance. Instead of saving money, managed competition would cost $270 billion over five years.

Mandatory employer-provided health insurance is also a non-solution to our health care spending and insurance problems. Plans being discussed in Washington would cause many employers to cut salaries or lay off workers, destroying in the process as many as 3.5 million jobs and reducing GNP by as much as $27 billion. Mandating insurance would cause rates and spending to rise still faster, perversely adding to the problem of the uninsured. Many employers would "dump" their less healthy employees into the public insurance program, increasing its costs and leading to more cost-shifting to privately insured patients.

Socialized medicine, a fourth non-solution, is no longer a popular proposal. But its ghost haunts plans for national health insurance by vividly revealing the long-term consequences of government control over health care. The British NHS has produced a dramatically lower quality of health care than is provided in the U.S. Long queues, denial of care to the elderly, and underinvestment in equipment and facilities are some of the problems that plague the system. A socialist health care system that is further down the road to disintegration is that of the Soviet Union. While some of the recent problems afflicting the Soviet health care system are a result of the general breakdown of the nation's socialist economy, many date back to a time when the system was operating as well as it historically ever had.

The failure of the Soviet, British, and Canadian health care systems to deliver quality services at affordable prices is leading policy makers in all those countries to abandon or alter their earlier models of socialist medicine and national health insurance. During the next five years, health care in each of these nations will come to resemble more closely the private-sector based, competitive U.S. system. Sadly, policy makers and opinion leaders in the U.S. seem oblivious to these changes in direction and the relevance of other countries' experiences to our own. As the rest of the world sets about "privatizing" its health care systems, only the U.S. seriously discusses pushing more of its largely private system into government hands.

CHAPTER SIX

Better Solutions

WHY DO WE spend too much on health care? Because the rise of government as the largest single buyer of health services has injected billions of dollars into the health care market while giving its beneficiaries few incentives to economize. In its role as tax collector, government encourages employers to provide their employees with low-deductible, low-copayment insurance policies, again fueling demand and diminishing incentives to comparison-shop and economize. Finally, in its role as regulator, government increases costs by mandating that insurers cover a wide range of conditions and treatments, limiting competition by enforcing Certificate of Need requirements, and preventing insurers and consumers from negotiating terms for managed care programs.

The unnecessarily high cost of health care and health insurance hurts us all. It makes our industries less competitive with those in countries where spending is lower. It means many people receive smaller paychecks and must pay for insurance coverage they do not need or use. For millions of Americans, high costs price them out of the market for health insurance, forcing them to rely on charitable care or the emergency rooms of public hospitals.

Individuals and organizations that promote national health insurance, managed competition, mandatory employer-provided insurance, or socialized medicine have overlooked the real causes of high spending. Their proposals bear little relevance to the actual causes of high spending, and consequently they have little hope of reducing costs or spending in the long term. These advocates also overlook the disturbing records of countries they hold up as models—countries that have tried national health insurance and socialized medicine and learned that these are not real solutions.

The policy changes needed to lower health care spending and improve access to care must address head-on the reasons for unnecessarily high spending. *They must put the individual consumer back into the center of the health care marketplace.* This can be done only by removing the distorting effects of federal tax policies and rules and regulations that needlessly increase the cost of supplying health care. "The solution," as Louise B. Russell wrote for The Brookings Institution fifteen years ago, "is to reintroduce some mechanism that will force those who make decisions about medical care to recognize that resources are costly and to weigh the costs against the benefits of any proposed action."[1]

A Fresh Start

REPEAL CURRENT REGULATION. No effort to reform the nation's health care system will succeed unless the many existing public policies that distort incentives and increase costs are removed. Instead of adding a new layer of regulation and bureaucracy on top of existing layers, the nation needs a fresh start. Following the analysis presented in Chapter Four, a fresh start requires:

■ Slowing the growth of federal and state health care entitlement programs in ways that do not result in cost-shifting to patients with private insurance;

■ Repeal of the 700 state laws mandating insurance coverage of specific conditions at a cost as high as $60 billion a year;

■ Repeal of Certificate of Need regulations and other restrictions on competition among hospitals and clinics;

■ Repeal of laws that limit the ability of insurers and

providers to form PPOs and other efforts to manage costs;

■ Dramatically shortening the current drug approval process that takes too long and costs too much to bring new drugs to market;

■ Repeal of occupational licensing laws, or at least their amendment to allow hospitals greater flexibility in defining the roles of licensed professionals.

TAX REFORM. Also critical to the success of health care reform is ending the incentives created by tax policy to rely too heavily on health insurance. As the table on page 63 demonstrated, the tax-favored status of employer-paid health insurance makes reliance on insurance, even expensive policies with very low deductibles, a bargain compared to buying health services with after-tax dollars. This unequal taxation of insurance and out-of-pocket spending on health care is, in the words of one expert, "the major inducement to over-insurance and over-consumption of health care in the U.S. Employees can launder ordinary health expenditures through 'insurance' and gain a discount equal to their marginal tax rate."[2] In an editorial endorsing a limit on the amount of tax-free health insurance premiums employees can receive, *The New York Times* said existing policy "encourages wasteful coverage" while a tax cap would "unleash the powerful competitive forces that will equip the consumer, and thus society, to make sensible choices about health care."[3]

    Taxing some employer-paid health insurance benefits is only half of the solution to putting insurance and out-of-pocket spending on an even footing. The other half is to extend the favorable tax treatment to persons who pay directly for health expenses. A plan that would do this is called Medical Savings Accounts (MSAs).[4] Under the MSA plan, employers could provide employees with insurance policies with high deductibles—catastrophic insurance—and pass along to employees the money saved on premiums. This money would be treated the same way as employer-paid insurance premiums are treated—that is, excluded from payroll taxes—provided it is deposited into Medical Savings Accounts (MSAs), similar to Individual Retirement Accounts (IRAs). Money would be allowed to accumulate in MSAs from year to year, and could be withdrawn only to pay for medical expenses.

Here is how the plan could work in practice.[5] An employer who now pays an average annual premium for family coverage of $4,500 per employee would replace that policy with a catastrophic policy having a deductible of $3,000 and costing $1,500 a year. The money saved by the change—$3,000—would be given directly to the employee to be deposited in a Medical Savings Account. The employee would deduct the $3,000 from his or her taxable income at the end of the year, just as is now done for deposits into IRAs, so money deposited into MSAs is treated the same as money spent buying insurance. The first $3,000 in medical expenses each year would be paid directly by the employee from the MSA, with insurance "kicking in" only to cover expenses above that level.

The theory behind the MSA plan is that the combination of a high deductible and a Medical Savings Account gives a health plan enrollee a direct financial incentive to avoid unnecessary utilization of health care services. Enrollees would be entering the health care marketplace spending their own money, not that of an anonymous insurance company. Any money left in the MSA at the end of the year would be allowed to accumulate over time, or it could be applied to non-medical expenses. (In the latter case, payroll taxes would have to be paid at the time of withdrawal.) Since two-thirds of families in America have medical expenses of under $3,000 a year, a significant majority of Americans would begin immediately to accumulate savings in Medical Savings Accounts.

How significantly would utilization fall if an MSA plan were implemented? According to the National Center for Policy Analysis, spending could fall by $90 billion to $147 billion a year.[6] Another $16 billion to $33 billion would be saved in administrative costs because insurance companies would no longer screen the first $3,000 in bills submitted.[7] Tax revenues lost by extending favorable tax treatment to MSAs could be offset by taxing employer-paid insurance premiums that exceed the amount necessary to buy a catastrophic insurance plan.

Many people who are now uninsured can afford to buy catastrophic insurance, but cannot afford to pay up to $3,000 a year in out-of-pocket expenses from their after-tax income. Under the MSA plan, such people could use *pre-tax* income to pay these expenses, effectively lowering their cost by nearly 50 percent. Those unable to afford catastrophic insurance or to make deposits into MSAs could receive tax credits and even public deposits into their MSAs, enabling them to participate in the program. As lower utilization and administrative costs gradually bring down the cost of health care and health insurance, more small employers and working poor would be able to afford policies. Many people would accumulate enough money in their Medical Savings Accounts to finance their greater health care needs as they grow older.

The Medical Savings Accounts plan has been endorsed by a long list of intellectuals, including Nobel Laureate Milton Friedman,[8] representatives of forty "think tanks,"[9] American Farm Bureau Federation, American Medical Association, National Federation of Independent Business, and others. Political figures as diverse as President George Bush and Senator Edward Kennedy have endorsed at least pilot MSA programs.

The NCPA Plan

In 1990, the Dallas-based NCPA assembled a national Health Care Task Force to address the problems of rising costs and growing numbers of uninsured. The resulting plan transfers power from large institutions and impersonal bureaucracies to individual health care consumers by restoring the buyer/seller relationship between patients and health care providers. By changing the tax treatment of individual health expenditures, the plan makes it more likely that patients will be spending their own money, rather than someone else's, when they purchase health care. The plan also exposes hospitals and other elements of the health care industry to the rigors of competition by repealing regulations and requiring that accurate price information be made available to patients.

The Health Care Task Force's recommendations, as they are summarized in the task force's report, follow.

1. Help Uninsured Individuals to Purchase Health Insurance.

COMMENT. Employees of large companies usually have health insurance exempt from costly state regulations and encouraged by generous provisions of the federal tax law. Individuals who purchase health insurance on their own, however, receive no tax encouragement and face premiums inflated by costly regulations. Public policy should be neutral with respect to the way in which individual insurance is purchased. We therefore recommend the following:

§ 1.A Allow insurers to sell no-frills, catastrophic health insurance not subject to state mandated benefits, premium taxes, risk pool assessments, and other costly regulations.

§ 1.B Allow individuals a tax credit for a portion of their health insurance premiums, so that individuals receive the same tax advantages available to employer-provided health insurance.

§ 1.C Make tax credits refundable for low-income families.

2. Encourage Employers to Provide Health Insurance for Employees.

COMMENT. Because of federal employee benefits laws, health benefits are individualized, but the costs are collectivized—a situation that encourages waste and discourages cost control. Small employers are further victimized by costly state regulations and federal laws that force them to create one-size-fits-all health insurance plans for all of their employees. These policies are encouraging large employers to limit coverage for employee dependents, and small employers to drop health insurance benefits altogether. We recommend the following:

§ 2.A Allow insurers to sell no-frills, catastrophic group insurance, not subject to costly state government regulations and taxes.

§ 2.B Make health insurance benefits part of the gross wage of employees and allow tax credits for premiums on individual tax returns, so that employees (rather than employers) bear the cost of waste and reap the benefits of prudence.

§ 2.C Allow each employee to choose a health insurance policy tailored to individual and family needs.

3. Eliminate Waste and Control Rising Health Care Costs.

COMMENT. The tax law contains generous encouragement for wasteful, first-dollar health insurance coverage under employer health care plans. There is no tax encouragement for individual self-insurance or allowing people to pay small medical bills with their own funds. Waste also occurs because most hospitals refuse to do for individual patients what they often do for government and large insurers—quote a single package price prior to admission. Patients cannot be prudent buyers in the hospital marketplace if they cannot compare prices. Medical costs are also rising because of an inefficient tort system. We recommend the following:

§ 3.A Limit favorable tax treatment for health insurance to catastrophic policies.

§ 3.B Allow each employee to choose between wages and health insurance coverage, so that employees who choose less expensive coverage will have more take-home pay.

§ 3.C Create tax credits for deposits to individual Medical Savings Accounts, from which people would use their own money to pay small medical expenses.

§ 3.D Require hospitals that accept government funds to negotiate a pre-admission package price with patients.

§ 3.E Allow patients to avoid the costly effects of the tort system through voluntary contract.

4. Encourage Saving for Post-retirement Health Care.

COMMENT. Although the tax law encourages virtually unlimited employer-provided health insurance coverage for current medical expenses, it provides little encouragement for employers and no encouragement for individuals to save for post-retirement medical needs. In both the public and private sectors, we are following a chain-letter approach to funding health care expenses for the elderly—an approach that will create an unbearable burden for future generations of workers. We recommend the following:

§ 4.A Create tax incentives for individuals and employers to save for post-retirement medical expenses.

§ 4.B Allow tax credits for individual or employer contributions to Medical IRA accounts designed to supplement and eventually replace coverage under Medicare.

5. Limit Waste in Medicare and Encourage Catastrophic Health Insurance for the Elderly.

COMMENT. Medicare pays too many small medical bills for the elderly while leaving them exposed to large, catastrophic medical expenses. Yet all attempts to resolve the problem through a one-size-fits-all health care plan have failed. We recommend the following:

§ 5.A Allow private insurers to repackage Medicare benefits and create diverse policies tailored to the different needs of Medicare beneficiaries.

§ 5.B Give the elderly tax incentives to self-insure through Medical Savings Accounts for small medical bills rather than rely on wasteful, third-party insurance coverage.

6. Avoid Rationing in the Medicare and Medicaid Programs.

COMMENT. Medicare (for the elderly) and Medicaid (for the poor) are becoming price-fixing schemes, administered by large, impersonal bureaucracies. Rather than empower patients in the medical marketplace, these programs increasingly limit access to medical care by regulating the terms and conditions under which medical services can be delivered. We recommend the following:

§ 6.A Medicaid patients should have the right to draw on an account, negotiate prices, and add their own money if necessary, in order to purchase certain types of medical services—particularly prenatal care.

§ 6.B For the categories of illness where it is apparent that Medicare is paying much less than the market price for reasonable care, Medicare patients should have the right to negotiate prices and supplement Medicare's payment with their own money or with private health insurance funds.

■   ■   ■

Adoption of the NCPA agenda would dramatically change the way health services are financed and delivered in the U.S. Here, briefly, is how a health care system restructured along these lines would work:

1) People who purchase health insurance with their own money, or who pay directly for health expenses, would receive a tax credit just as valuable as tax subsidies to employer-provided health insurance. Employees who receive low-deductible, low-copayment, high-premium insurance policies from their employers would pay taxes on part of the premiums.

2) People would save for medical expenses through individual Medical Savings Accounts. Deposits to such accounts would be tax deductible and interest would be tax exempt. A sizable portion of the money deposited in these accounts could come from savings resulting from insurance policies with higher deductibles and copayment requirements.

3) Over time, Medical Savings Account balances would grow and people would rely on health insurance only for very large medical bills, returning insurance to its original function of insuring against unforeseen tragedies instead of pre-payment of expected medical expenses. Individuals will have regained control over their medical spending.

4) Hospitals would be required to negotiate pre-admission prices with patients and give patients information about the quality of their services. This allows patients, who will now have incentives to comparison-shop, to compare prices offered by competing providers.

5) The variety of insurance policies available to individuals would be expanded by allowing people to purchase no-frills, catastrophic health insurance, and allowing employers to offer employees a variety of health insurance plans. The cross-subsidies inherent in a "one-size-fits-all" insurance policy would be eliminated, making insurance attractive to many young and healthy people who now are uninsured by choice.

6) Everyone could make tax-deductible contributions to a medical IRA to cover medical expenses in their old age. Private insurers would be allowed to repackage Medicare benefits and

sell a variety of insurance policies to meet the different needs of Medicare beneficiaries.

The ALEC Plan

The American Legislative Exchange Council (ALEC) is the nation's largest voluntary membership organization for state legislators. In late 1991, it drew on its extensive membership to begin drafting a comprehensive agenda on health care issues. So far, the plan has five components: insurance reform, Medicaid privatization, medical liability reform, creation of new long-term care alternatives, and incentives to promote rural health care. The summary presented below is based on subcommittee reports presented in December 1991.

1. Make Insurance More Affordable, Accessible, and Portable.

MISSION STATEMENT. To give 100 percent of the population maximum access to quality cost-effective health care.

§ 1.A Extend tax credits or deductions to individuals who buy health insurance and to those without insurance who pay medical expenses out-of-pocket. Allow individuals to create Medical Savings Accounts from which to pay directly small medical expenses.

§ 1.B Repeal state mandates that require health insurers to cover uncommon conditions and treatments.

§ 1.C Repeal laws that limit the right of insurers to select providers with whom they contract or limit the range of financial incentives given to insureds to use one provider over another.

§ 1.D Require providers to increase the supply of information given to patients, and repeal Certificate Of

Need (CON) regulations.

§ 1.E Make small group health insurance *collectively renewable.* Require that each carrier's entire book of small group businesses be pooled so that no small group can be singled out for termination due to health, claim cost, or length of time of coverage. Limit the amount an insurer can annually raise rates for any given group due to health, claim cost, or length of time of coverage. Limit the difference that two similar groups can pay for similar coverage for these same reasons.

§ 1.F Give each person covered by a small group plan the right to convert to a permanent individual health insurance plan with benefits identical to those of the original plan, and limit the premium for the new plan to a small surcharge over the original rate.

§ 1.G Guarantee that anyone who has remained in the health insurance system be covered with no new limitations as a new addition to an employer's group health insurance plan. Together, recommendations 1.F and 1.G mean no one can fall out of the health insurance system through no fault of his own or be locked into a job for fear of losing access to health insurance.

§ 1.H Guarantee that a group with coverage will be treated as a whole group if it changes insurance carriers or coverage. The group will not face any exclusions or new limitations; thus, "cherry-picking" is eliminated.

§ 1.I Guarantee that no group can be denied coverage due simply to the nature of its business, and limit to reasonable levels any "nature of business" surcharges.

§ 1.J Remove from the employer-based insurance system the 1 to 2 percent of the population that is uninsurable or insurable only at extremely high rates. Create state-funded comprehensive high risk pools (CHIPs) and set premium rates at 150 percent of a standard rate charged for comparable coverage in the state to avoid competition with other carriers.

2. Privatize Medicaid Through the Use of Vouchers.

MISSION STATEMENT. Privatize Medicaid through the use of vouchers and create a program that would decrease state expenditures, streamline state Medicaid programs, and provide access to health care to a greater number of needy families.

§ 2.A Medicaid would be limited to AFDC recipients, beginning at 100 percent of the poverty level.

§ 2.B Each eligible Medicaid AFDC recipient would receive a voucher for a specified amount to purchase a family health care policy. Each voucher would be used to purchase a certified health insurance policy through a risk underwriting entity and/or organized health care system.

§ 2.C Each health insurance policy would exclude deductibles, copayments, and state mandatory benefits, but would include the nine federal Medicaid mandates plus 30 days inpatient care for mental health, mental retardation, and substance abuse; prescription drugs; lifestyle incentives for preventive education; and prenatal care coverage.

§ 2.D Persons deemed uninsurable would be covered by existing risk pools or insurers of last resort. Program savings would be directed toward expanded eligibility for Medicaid coverage.

3. Reform Medical Liability to Reduce Litigation Costs.

MISSION STATEMENT. To reform liability laws in a way that ensures that litigation is initiated only in response to illegal, unethical, or negligent medical practices or civil or criminal actions, not unavoidable risks.

§ 3.A Cap non-economic medical malpractice damages at $250,000 or five times actual damages.

§ 3.B Eliminate joint and several liability for non-economic medical malpractice damages.

§ 3.C Allow periodic rather than lump-sum payment of punitive awards and future medical costs greater than $50,000.

§ 3.D Develop guidelines for state medical licensing boards that require lay persons on the board, mechanisms for the state to inform other states of medical providers who have lost their licenses or had their licenses suspended, provide immunity from civil liability for "whistle-blowers," and streamline disciplinary processes.

§ 3.E Extend liability immunity for health care professionals who are on call without compensation to a hospital emergency room, personnel performing medical or dental treatment without compensation at nonprofit clinics, physicians under contract to provide obstetrical services to indigent patients (such physicians are to be considered state employees and as such are protected against individual liability exposure), and persons providing emergency obstetrical care to a woman in active labor when the person does not have access to the patient's medical records.

§ 3.F Reestablish community standards by authorizing the creation of Community Standard Development Committees (CSDC), approved by the State Health Care Information Agency, to define service areas and approved community standard procedures. Health care providers following an approved community standard procedure would be immune from any finding of negligence in a malpractice claim.

§ 3.G Develop alternative dispute resolution mechanisms, either voluntary nonbinding arbitration or voluntary mediation, as the first response to patient/provider conflicts.

4. Provide Better Alternatives and Options for Financing Long-Term Care.

MISSION STATEMENT. Provide better alternatives and options for financing and arranging long-term care by discouraging asset sheltering and encouraging innovation and flexibility in health insurance policies.

§ 4.A Forbid wealthy, elderly individuals from sheltering assets in order to qualify for Medicare benefits. Appropriate legislation should enable states, like any other responsible creditor, to take available legal measures to protect their recovery interest.

§ 4.B Pass legislation permitting elderly homeowners to meet their financial needs through "reverse mortgages," giving them access to the equity in their homes.

§ 4.C Pass legislation promoting the availability of long-term care insurance policies by establishing standards and facilitating flexibility and innovation in the development of insurance coverage.

5. Expand and Improve Rural Health Care Services.

MISSION STATEMENT. To deliver essential health care to rural areas by attracting providers through incentives, waivers, and use of specially trained midlevel care professionals, and by allowing existing facilities to redesign themselves into service centers that offer restricted services without sacrificing minimum levels of preventative, primary, and emergency care.

§ 5.A Allow and encourage greater use of midlevel professionals: physician assistants, nurse practitioners, nurse midwives, etc.

§ 5.B Waive federal and state reimbursement and licensure requirements to allow the creation of rural health clinics, primary care hospitals, medical assistance facilities, and alternative rural hospitals. Allow existing facilities to redesign their services without sacrificing minimum levels of preventative, primary and emergency care.

§ 5.C Make use of incentive options, including reimbursement incentives, tuition loan forgiveness, and special indemnification to attract health practitioners to rural communities.

■   ■   ■

The ALEC plan addresses high health insurance costs in some of the same ways as the NCPA plan, but it adds further reforms to bring costs under control. Its reforms to small group insurance would expand coverage in this important area, and liability reform would reduce the tremendous expenses caused by misuse of the tort system and defensive medicine. The recommendations on rural health care acknowledge that state and federal regulations governing reimbursement under Medicaid and certification of facilities often stand in the way of providing affordable health care in remote areas. By clearing away these regulations, the ALEC plan lowers costs and increases access to care.

Conclusion

The promise of the NCPA and ALEC plans is apparent if one considers the enormous costs they would remove from the shoulders of American health care consumers. By repealing state insurance mandates, the plans would reduce insurance costs by as much as 30 percent, some 10 percent of total health care spending. By extending favorable tax treatment to insurance premiums and medical expenses paid directly by individuals, the plans reduce by as much as 50 percent the effective price of health insurance for many of the currently uninsured. By limiting the tax exclusion to catastrophic insurance, the NCPA plan dramatically reduces the tax subsidy to low-deductible, low-copayment insurance plans, bringing to a quick end expensive first-dollar policies.

With the change to insurance plans with higher deductibles and copayments, the emergence of tax-sheltered Medical Savings Accounts from which individuals can pay their own medical expenses, and tax credits for people with low incomes, millions of Americans would for the first time have reason to act as careful consumers of health care services. The Rand experiment described in Chapter 4 suggests people would react immediately by cutting back on unnecessary utilization of health care, saving billions of dollars more each year. As consumers are armed with price information produced by competing hospitals, a genuine marketplace for health care would reemerge. The value that people place on health services would be reflected in the prices they are willing to pay . . . prices that would be lower because of the newly competitive market, but payments that would be more dear because they come from one's own Medical Savings Account.

The proposals made by ALEC to privatize Medicaid and by NCPA to privatize Medicare would further drive the health care system toward efficiency and accountability. Allowing private insurance companies to write policies for the 57 million people insured by Medicaid and Medicare would empower these people to choose plans tailored to their needs and put an immediate end to cost-shifting caused by underpayment by the federal government to health care providers. *Imagine the effect of 57 million people who now must depend on the whims of the Medicaid and Medicare bureaucracies suddenly being given the power to choose their insurer or pay small medical bills from their own accounts!* Billions more would be saved by the elimination of the bureaucracy that has accompanied the federal government's DRG program, and the "regulatory nightmare" promised by the new set of regulations concerning doctors' fees.

The small group insurance reforms proposed by ALEC would make affordable health insurance available to more small businesses. Its series of guarantees ensure that insurance is maintained when the link to a particular employer is broken by job changes, retirement, divorce, or death. More individuals will choose to be insured, and more small businesses will provide insurance, if they are guaranteed insurability, fairness, and portability of insurance once they enter the system.

The high risk pools proposed by ALEC solve the last remaining problem: providing reliable access to care for those presently without health insurance and with pre-existing health problems so severe that no insurer will write an affordable policy. The ALEC solution is to remove these people from the insurance system—for they are in fact *uninsurable*—and arrange for their treatment to be funded by broad-based taxes or assessments. If such a plan were used in combination with tax credits, people with chronic, uninsurable conditions would find quality care that is also affordable.

This is an exciting vision of reform and consumer empowerment. It promises to save tens of billions of dollars a year in health care spending *without* rationing care, underinvesting in technology or facilities, or any of the other drawbacks that plague national health insurance plans. Most importantly, the NCPA and ALEC proposals enable us to find the best level of health care and the "right" price. They do so by freeing individual health care consumers to make their own judgments and decisions about when to buy, how much to buy, and how much to pay.

This reform agenda is more complicated, and perhaps less attractive as a result, than calls for "comprehensive restructuring" or adoption of "the Canadian Model." Recent polls suggest that the rhetoric of nationalization advocates has won over a substantial part of the American public. But perhaps the American people know better than to accept at face value proposals that promise simple solutions to complicated problems. Perhaps, if informed of the true nature of the problem and the true cost of national health insurance and socialized medicine in other nations, the American people will listen to and embrace an alternative reform agenda with greater promise.

CHAPTER SEVEN

Where We Go From Here

WHILE SOME of the ideas put forward in this book are new, many have been advanced for several years by influential and respected researchers and political leaders. The leaders of the two major political parties have said they will pursue an "incremental" reform agenda rather than endorse sweeping reorganization, a sign perhaps that the NCPA and ALEC agendas are being taken seriously in Washington. But the forces opposed to realistic reform are extremely powerful. Unless thousands of concerned citizens make their opinions heard, the promising reforms described in Chapter 6 may never get a fair hearing.

What You Can Do

1. **Write and call your state legislator, Congressman, and Senators.**

Letters to elected officials *are* read, and they can have a major influence on the legislative process. Many elected officials say that if they receive just *twenty* letters on a given subject, they feel they must respond to their constituents' concerns. If you do not know who your elected representatives are, call your local public library or board of elections.

When you contact these officials, tell them you are aware of the problems of high health care spending and the growing number of people lacking insurance, but you do not believe the solution lies in national health insurance, managed competition, mandatory employer-provided insurance, or socialized medicine. Tell them you support proposals containing the money-saving and consumer-empowering provisions of the NCPA and ALEC plans. Ask them to examine these proposals seriously and support them when the issues come before them in meetings or for votes.

2.   Learn more about the issues.

There are many excellent books and shorter publications addressing health care spending, the problem of the uninsured, and the solutions that are needed. Here are some that we specifically recommend:

An Agenda for Solving America's Health Care Crisis, by the NCPA Health Care Task Force (Dallas, TX: National Center for Policy Analysis, 1990), 33 pp.

The ALEC Health Care Reform Proposal, by the ALEC National Task Force on Health Care (Washington, DC: American Legislative Exchange Council, 1992).

Controlling Health Care Costs with Medical Savings Accounts, by John C. Goodman and Gerald L. Musgrave (Dallas, TX: National Center for Policy Analysis, 1992), 40 pp.

Health Care in America: The Political Economy of Hospitals and Health Insurance, edited by H.E. Frech III (San Francisco, CA: Pacific Research Institute, 1988), 401 pp.

A National Health System for America, edited by Stuart M. Butler and Edmund F. Haislmaier (Washington, DC: The Heritage Foundation, 1989), 127 pp.

Freedom of Choice in Health Insurance, by John C. Goodman and Gerald L. Musgrave (Dallas, TX: National Center for Policy Analysis, November 1988), 36 pp.

3.   **Buy multiple copies of this book for your friends and neighbors.**

This book can serve as a conversation starter or even a point of departure for the formation of a local pro-consumer and pro-choice health care reform group. If you thought it helped give you the facts and information you need to take a position in the public debate, then consider giving copies to your friends and neighbors. Most people will read a book if someone they know recommends it or gives it to them as a gift.

4.   **Support organizations that are fighting for responsible health care reform.**

The organizations that developed the NCPA and ALEC plans and produced this book are supported by individual, corporate, and foundation contributions. They rely on voluntary aid from people like you to continue their work. Contributions are tax deductible as charitable gifts. The groups can be contacted at:

National Center for Policy Analysis
12655 North Central Expressway, Suite 720
Dallas, Texas   75243
214/386-6272

American Legislative Exchange Council
214 Massachusetts Avenue, N.E.
Washington, DC   20002
202/547-4646

The Heartland Institute - Chicago
P.O. Box 2708
Chicago, Illinois   60690-2708
312/427-3060

The Heartland Institute also has offices in Milwaukee, Wisconsin;

Detroit, Michigan; Cleveland, Ohio; St. Louis, Missouri; and Kansas City, Missouri. Information and additional copies of this book can be obtained by contacting any of these offices.

A Parting Thought

Early in this book we described the "subjective" nature of values and how this made comparisons of health care costs and spending extremely difficult. Each person places his or her own value on health and health care, just as he or she independently values every other good and service. Because valuing is a private affair, we ought to respect every person's judgment of value, and consequently his or her right to choose among available options.

The current debate over health care reform has a lot to do with respecting other people's judgments. Some of the reforms being advocated—national health insurance, managed competition, mandatory employer-provided insurance, and socialized medicine —would immediately take away freedoms Americans have come to expect. In the long run, we believe these "reforms" would result in even greater restrictions on personal choice, and as a result, less valuable outcomes for most people.

If you believe the solution to America's health care problems is to be found in empowering consumers—by expanding choice and removing distorting subsidies, taxes, and regulations— please make your voice heard today. Those who do not respect your right to choose dominate the public debate . . . and they will succeed in limiting your freedom *unless you act now.*

Endnotes

Introduction

1. See the newsletters of the National Association of Manufacturers, particularly *Briefing*, Volume XVI, No. 21, August 5, 1991; and Charles P. Hall, Jr. and John M. Kuder, "Small Business and Health Care: Results of a Survey" (Washington, DC: The NFIB Foundation, April 1990), page 13.

2. "Access to Health Care," *Annals of Internal Medicine*, Volume 112, No. 9, May 1, 1990.

3. See Alain C. Enthoven, "What Can Europeans Learn from Americans?" *Health Care Financing Review*, Annual Supplement 1989, page 49. Regarding the question asked in the title of his essay, Enthoven says "the obvious answer is 'not much.'"

4. General Accounting Office, *Canadian Health Insurance: Lessons for the United States* (Washington, DC: U.S. Government Printing Office, June 1991).

5. Conventional wisdom often mirrors the self-interests of industry groups. The American College of Physicians, for example, has focused public attention on the administrative costs of hospitals and insurance companies, but is silent about the effects of laws that limit competition among hospitals and restrict lower-cost alternative health care methods.

Chapter One
What Do We Mean By "Too Much"?

1. "States Take Lead in Health Reform," *Nation's Business*, April 1992, page 18.

2. Shelda Harden, "Confronting the Health Care Crisis," *State Legislatures*, June 1991, page 33.

3. See Jack Meyer, Sharon Silow-Carroll, and Sean Sullivan, *Critical Choice Confronting the Cost of American Health Care* (Washington, DC: National Committee for Quality Health Care, 1990), page 30; and "Health Care's Road to Recovery: Address the Cost and Access Problems Now,"

Special Report (Washington, DC: U.S. Chamber of Commerce, September 23, 1991).

4. "You Bet Your Life," *The Economist*, October 27, 1990, page 14.

5. Shelda Harden, supra note 2.

6. Ibid.

7. Charles P. Hall, Jr. and John M. Kuder, "Small Business and Health Care: Results of a Survey" (Washington, DC: The NFIB Foundation, April 1990).

8. Henry J. Aaron, *Serious and Unstable Condition: Financing America's Health Care* (Washington, DC: The Brookings Institution, 1991), page 102.

9. Alain C. Enthoven and Richard Kronick, "A Consumer-Choice Health Plan for the 1990s," *New England Journal of Medicine*, 320:29-37, January 5, 1989, page 29.

10. "Health Care Reform: The Time is Now!" American Association of Retired Persons, 1991, page 3.

11. Jim Abrams, "National health plan advanced by business, labor, consumers," *Chicago Sun Times*, November 13, 1991.

12. U.S. Chamber of Commerce, supra note 3, page 1.

13. Henry J. Aaron, supra note 8, page 142.

14. Armen Alchian and William R. Allen, *Exchange and Production: Competition, Coordination, and Control*, 2nd edition (Belmont, CA: Wadsworth Publishing Company, 1977), page 13.

15. John Goodman, "Beware of National Health Insurance," *The Heritage Lectures* (Washington, DC: The Heritage Foundation, May 17, 1990), page 2.

16. Henry J. Aaron, supra note 8, pages 87, 104.

17. Robert J. Gordon, *Macroeconomics* (Boston, MA: Little, Brown and Company, 1978), first appendix; Rudiger Dornbusch and Stanley Fischer, *Macroeconomics* (New York, NY: McGraw-Hill Book Company, 1978), page 28; Osker Morgenstern, *On the Accuracy of Economic Observations* (Princeton, NJ: Princeton University Press, 1965); and National Bureau of Economic Research, *A Critique of the U.S. Income and Product Accounts* (Princeton, NJ: Princeton University Press, 1958).

18. George J. Schieber and Jean-Pierre Poullier, "Overview of international comparisons of health care expenditures," *Health Care Financing Review*, Annual Supplement 1989, page 1. See also the disclaimer in International Hospital Federation, *A Guide to Health Services of the World* (Great Britain: International Hospital Federation, 1990).

19. Dale A. Rublee and Markus Schneider, "International Health Spending: Comparisons with the OECD," *Health Affairs*, Fall 1991, pages 187-188.

20. See Joseph P. Newhouse, "Measuring Medical Prices and Understanding Their Effects: The Baxter Foundation Prize Address," *Journal of Health Administration Education*, Vol. 7, Winter 1989, pages 19-26; Fred R. Glahe, *Macroeconomics: Theory and Policy* (New York, NY: Harcourt Brace Jovanovich, Inc., 1973), page 12; and Henry J. Aaron, supra note 8, pages 103-107.

21. Victor R. Fuchs, *Who Shall Live?* (New York, NY: Basic Books, Inc., 1974), page 12.

22. National Bureau of Economic Research, supra note 17, page 7.

23. For an excellent overview of subjectivism in modern economics, see *Method, Process, and Austrian Economics*, edited by Israel Kirzner (Lexington, MA: Lexington Books, 1983).

24. Ludwig von Mises, *Human Action* (Chicago, IL: Contemporary Books, Inc., 1949), page 217.

25. Friedrich Hayek, *Individual and Economic Order* (Chicago, IL: Henry Regnery Company, 1948 (Gateway edition, 1972)).

26. James M. Buchanan and Gordon Tullock, *The Calculus of Consent* (Ann Arbor, MI: University of Michigan Press, 1962), and *Public Finance in Democratic Process* (Chapel Hill, NC: University of North Carolina Press, 1967).

27. Victor R. Fuchs, supra note 21, pages 27-28; and Lynn Payer, *Medicine and Culture: Varieties of Treatment in the U.S., England, West Germany, and France* (New York, NY: Henry Holt and Company, 1988), page 70.

28. Princeton University economist Timothy Besley summarizes the results of 15 econometric studies, all of them showing a downward sloping demand curve for health care, in "The Demand for Health Care and Health Insurance," in *Providing Health Care: The Economics of Alternative Systems of Finance and Delivery*, edited by Alistair McGuire, Paul Fenn, and Kenneth Mayhew (Oxford: Oxford University Press, 1991), pages 51-52; see also Willard G. Manning et al., "Health Insurance and the Demand for Medical Care: Evidence from a Randomized Experiment," *American Economic Review*, 77:3, June 1987, pages 251-277.

Chapter Two
International Comparisons

1. Henry J. Aaron, *Serious and Unstable Condition: Financing America's Health Care* (Washington, DC: The Brookings Institution, 1991), page 1.

2. Victor R. Fuchs, *Who Shall Live?* (New York, NY: Basic Books, Inc., 1974), page 6.

3. Roger Formisano, "A Briefing on Health Care Issues" (Madison, WI: University of Wisconsin Center for Health Care Fiscal Management, 1989).

4. See Alain C. Enthoven, "What Can Europeans Learn from Americans?" *Health Care Financing Review*, Annual Supplement 1989.

5. Edward Neuschler, "Canadian Health Care: The Implications of Public Health Insurance," *Research Bulletin* (Washington, DC: The Health Insurance Association of America, June 1990), page 2.

6. GNP—Gross National Product—is different from, but in most important ways comparable to, GDP (Gross Domestic Product).

7. The Organization for Economic Cooperation and Development (OECD) developed and regularly updates the purchasing power parity (PPP) index.

8. Henry J. Aaron, supra note 1, page 107.

Chapter Three
Why Health Care Costs Are So High

1. A.J. Culyer, "Cost Containment in Europe," *Health Care Financing Review*, Annual Supplement 1989, page 23.

2. George J. Schieber and Jean-Pierre Poullier, "Overview of international comparisons of health care expenditures," *Health Care Financing Review*, Annual Supplement 1989, page 172.

3. Center for Health Policy Research, American Medical Association, "Chartbook of Cross-National Health Care Comparison: Demographics, Expenditures, Utilization, and Resources," December 1989.

4. Lynn Payer, *Medicine and Culture: Varieties of Treatment in the U.S., England, West Germany, and France* (New York, NY: Henry Holt and Company, 1988), page 70.

5. Ibid., pages 102-103.

6. Ibid., page 124.

7. Clyde McAvoy, "Health Care: Does America Pay Too Much?" *Business Tokyo*, August 1990, page 10.

8. Alf Siewers, "Don't socialize U.S. medicine, Sullivan says," *Chicago Sun-Times*, June 24, 1991.

9. Leonard A. Sagan, *The Health of Nations: True Causes of Sickness and Well-Being* (New York, NY: Basic Books, Inc., 1987).

10. Nicholas Eberstadt, "Why Are So Many American Babies Dying?" *The American Enterprise*, September/October 1991, page 38.

11. Robin Herman, "Diseases of Affluence," *Washington Post*, January 3, 1989.

12. Alain C. Enthoven and Richard Kronick, "A Consumer-Choice Health Plan for the 1990s," *New England Journal of Medicine*, 320:29-31, January 5, 1989, page 30.

13. Victor R. Fuchs, *Who Shall Live?* (New York, NY: Basic Books, Inc., 1974), page 30ff; and Leonard A. Sagan, supra note 9.

14. Leonard A. Sagan, supra note 9, page 74.

15. Leroy L. Schwartz, "The Medical Costs of America's Social Ills," *Wall Street Journal*, June 24, 1991.

16. Dr. Beny Primm, "Drug Abuse and Inner City Health Care," *The Heritage Lectures* #297 (Washington, DC: The Heritage Foundation, 1991), pages 66-72.

17. Joan Beck, "Public hospitals' safety net wearing dangerously thin," *Chicago Tribune*, January 31, 1991.

18. Carolyn Skorneck, "Hospitals record drop in drug-related visits," *Chicago Sun-Times*, July 3, 1991.

19. C.S. Phibbs, D.A. Bateman, and R.M. Schwartz, "The Neonatal Costs of Maternal Cocaine Use," *Journal of the American Medical Association*, Vol. 266, No. 11, September 18, 1991, pages 1521-1526.

20. Leroy L. Schwartz, supra note 15, estimates $63,000 per baby for the first five years.

21. Ibid.

22. William Winkerwerder, Austin R. Kellser, and Rhonda M. Stolec, "Federal Spending for Illness Caused by the Human Immuno-deficiency Virus," *New England Journal of Medicine*, June 15, 1989, pages 1598-1603.

23. Ernle W.D. Young and David K. Stevenson, "Limiting Treatment for Extremely Premature Low-Birthweight Infants (500 to 750g)," *American Journal of Diseases of Children*, Vol. 144, May 1990, pages 549-552.

24. Quoted in Stuart A. Wesbury, Jr., "Why Other Nations' R$_x$ Won't Work," *Healthcare Executive*, Vol. 5, No. 4, July/August 1990, page 18. See also Ernle W.D. Young and David K. Stevenson, ibid.

25. Center for Health Policy Research, supra note 3, page 6.

26. Nicholas Eberstadt, supra note 10, pages 39-40. Eberstadt also points out that other countries probably significantly undercount infant deaths. See also Victor R. Fuchs, *Who Shall Live?*, supra note 13, pages 31-33.

27. Cited in General Accounting Office, *Canadian Health Insurance:*

Lessons for the United States (Washington, DC: U.S. Government Printing Office, June 1991), page 17.

28. Nicholas Eberstadt, supra note 10, page 40.

29. Center for Health Policy Research, supra note 3, page 5.

30. Jacob S. Siegel and Maria Davidson, "Demographic and Socioeconomic Aspects of Aging in the United States," U.S. Department of Commerce, Bureau of the Census, Special Studies, August 1984, page 73.

31. Ibid.

32. Jack Meyer, Sharon Silow-Carroll, and Sean Sullivan, *Critical Choice Confronting the Cost of American Health Care* (Washington, DC: National Committee for Quality Health Care, 1990), page 52.

33. Victor R. Fuchs, "Though Much Is Taken: Reflections on Aging, Health, and Medical Care," *Milbank Memorial Fund Quarterly/Health and Society* 62 No. 2, 1984, pages 143-166.

34. Jacques Kransy and Ian R. Ferrier, "Canadian Healthcare System in Perspective," Bogart Delefield Ferrier, Inc., July 1990.

35. Dale A. Rublee, "Medical Technology in Canada, Germany, and the United States," *Health Affairs*, Fall 1989, page 180.

36. Jeffrey N. Gibbs, "Will the Safe Medical Devices Act Impede the Quality of Health Care?" *Legal Backgrounder*, Volume 6, No. 22 (Washington, DC: Washington Legal Foundation, June 28, 1991).

37. Jacques Kransy and Ian R. Ferrier, supra note 34.

38. William B. Schwartz, "The Inevitable Failure of Current Cost-Containment Strategies," *Journal of the American Medical Association*, Vol. 257, No. 2, January 9, 1987, pages 220-224.

39. Victor R. Fuchs, "Learning from the Canadian Experience," *Health Affairs*, Winter 1988, page 28.

40. Dale A. Rublee, supra note 35, page 181.

41. Ernle W.D. Young and David K. Stevenson, supra note 23.

42. General Accounting Office, supra note 27.

43. Spencer Rich, "Study Cites Cost of 'Defensive Medicine'" *Chicago Sun-Times*, February 3, 1993.

44. Ibid.

45. Jennifer F. Reinganum and Louis L. Wilde, "Settlement, Litigation, and the Allocation of Legal Costs," *Rand Journal of Economics*, Vol. 17, 1986.

46. Peter Huber, "Malpractice Law—A Defective Product," *Forbes*, April 16, 1990, page 154.

47. William M. Landes and Richard A. Posner, "Legal Precedent: A

Theoretical and Empirical Analysis," *Journal of Law and Economics*, Vol. 19, 1976, pages 249-307.

Chapter Four
Why We Spend Too Much

1. *Statistical Abstract of the U.S.*, 1989, Table 158.

2. Ibid.

3. See Alain C. Enthoven and Richard Kronick, "A Consumer-Choice Health Plan for the 1990s," *New England Journal of Medicine* 320:29-37, January 5, 1989, for source citations.

4. William B. Schwartz, "The Inevitable Failure of Current Cost-Containment Strategies," *Journal of the American Medical Association*, Vol. 257, No. 2, January 9, 1987, page 222.

5. Jack Meyer, Sharon Silow-Carroll, and Sean Sullivan, *Critical Choice Confronting the Cost of American Health Care* (Washington, DC: National Committee for Quality Health Care, 1990), page 30.

6. The ideas in this section have a long history and many prominent exponents. See Martin S. Feldstein, *The Rising Cost of Hospital Care* (Washington, DC: Information Resources Press, 1971); Martin S. Feldstein, *Hospital Costs and Health Insurance* (Cambridge, MA: Harvard University Press, 1981); Peter Temin, "An Economic History of American Hospitals," in *Health Care in America*, edited by H.E. Frech III (San Francisco, CA: Pacific Research Institute, 1988), pages 75-102; Aldona Robbins, Gary Robbins, and John C. Goodman, "Employee Benefits Law: The Case for Radical Reform" (Dallas, TX: Center for Health Policy Studies, National Center for Policy Analysis, March 1990); and Stuart M. Butler, "A Tax Reform Strategy to Deal With the Uninsured," *Journal of the American Medical Association*, Vol. 265, No. 19, May 15, 1991, pages 2541-2544.

7. H.E. Frech III, "Monopoly in Health Insurance: The Economics of Kartell v. Blue Shield of Massachusetts," in *Health Care in America*, edited by H.E. Frech III (San Francisco, CA: Pacific Research Institute, 1988), page 313.

8. Charles P. Hall, Jr. and John M. Kuder, "Small Business and Health Care: Results of a Survey" (Washington, DC: The NFIB Foundation, April 1990), page 2.

9. Louise B. Russell, "Medical Care Costs," in *Setting National Priorities: The 1978 Budget*, edited by Joseph A. Pechman (Washington, DC: The Brookings Institution, 1977), page 182.

10. *Chicago Tribune*, October 18, 1990.

11. Willard G. Manning et al., "Health Insurance and the Demand for Medical Care: Evidence from a Randomized Experiment," *American Economic Review*, 77:3, June 1987, pages 251-277.

12. Aldona Robbins, Gary Robbins, and John C. Goodman, supra note 6.

13. See, for example, Sidney Marchasin, "One Hospital Tells the Cost of Regulation," *Wall Street Journal*, June 26, 1990.

14. Julie Kosterlitz, "A Brave New World for Doctors," *National Journal*, June 8, 1991, page 1367.

15. Robert E. Moffit, "Comparable Worth for Doctors: A Severe Case of Government Malpractice," *Backgrounder* (Washington, DC: The Heritage Foundation, September 23, 1991), page 22.

16. Jack Meyer, Sharon Silow-Carroll, and Sean Sullivan, supra note 5, pages 46-47.

17. John C. Goodman, "How to Help America's Uninsured," *Consumers' Research*, August 1990, page 13.

18. John C. Goodman and Gerald Musgrave, "Freedom of Choice in Health Insurance," *Policy Report* (Dallas, TX: National Center for Policy Analysis, November 1988).

19. Ibid. For a recent restatement, see John C. Goodman, "Health Insurance: States Can Help," *Wall Street Journal*, December 17, 1991.

20. Monica Noether, *Competition Among Hospitals*, Staff Report of the Bureau of Economics, Federal Trade Commission, 1987; David S. Salkever and Thomas W. Bice, *Hospital Certificate-of-Need Controls: Impact on Investment, Costs, and Use* (Washington, DC: American Enterprise Institute, 1979); Frank A. Sloan and Bruce Steinwald, "Effects of Regulation on Hospital Costs and Input Use," *Journal of Law and Economics*, April 1980, page 105.

21. David Burda, "CONspiracies to crush competition," *Modern Healthcare*, July 8, 1991, page 28.

22. Jack Meyer, Sharon Silow-Carroll, and Sean Sullivan, supra note 5, page 57; Wyatt Company, "Cost Analysis of State Legislative Mandates on Six Managed Health Care Practices," 1991.

23. Jack Meyer, Sharon Silow-Carroll, and Sean Sullivan, supra note 5, page 58.

24. R. Brown, et al., *The Value of Pharmaceuticals: A Study of Selected Conditions to Measure the Contribution of Pharmaceuticals to Health Status* (Seattle, WA: Battelle Medical Technology Assessment and Policy Research Center, March 1990).

25. Per-capita expenditures were $182 for the U.S., compared to $187 for Canada, $321 for Germany, $201 for Britain, and $218 for an average of

23 OECD countries. George J. Schieber, Jean-Pierre Poullier, and Leslie M. Greenwald, "Health Care Systems in Twenty-Four Countries," *Health Affairs*, Fall 1991, page 33.

26. David Leo Weimer, "Safe—and Available—Drugs," in *Instead of Regulation: Alternatives to Federal Regulatory Agencies*, edited by Robert W. Poole, Jr. (Lexington, MA: Lexington Books, 1982), page 241.

27. Ibid., page 239.

28. Eli Lilly and Co., 1992 first quarter report, page 4; Regina E. Herzlinger, *Creating New Health Care Ventures: The Role of Management* (Gaithersburg, NY: Aspen Publishers, Inc., 1992), page 36.

29. The average cost of reviewing a request under an Arkansas Medicaid program was $22.36, while the average cost of the prescriptions being reviewed was just $13.34. The program was eventually abandoned. See "Drug Costs Doubled Under Controversial Program," *Arkansas Times*, September 10, 1992.

30. Mitch Daniels, Vice President, Eli Lilly and Co., *White House Bulletin* (Alexandria, VA: Bulletin Broadfaxing Network, December 8, 1992), page 6.

31. Milton Friedman, *Capitalism and Freedom* (Chicago, IL: University of Chicago Press, 1962), page 158; Reuben Kessel, "The A.M.A. and the Supply of Physicians," *Journal of Law and Contemporary Problems*, 1970, pages 267-279; and Simon Rottenberg, editor, *Occupational Licensure and Regulation* (Washington, DC: American Enterprise Institute, 1980).

32. Stanley Gross, *Of Foxes and Henhouses* (Westport, CT: Quorum Books, 1984); Robert O. Becker, MD, and Gary Selden, *The Body Electric* (Quill, 1985); and David Scott Lynn, "Occupational Licensing," in *Coming Out of the Ice: A Plan to Make the 1990s Illinois' Decade*, edited by Joseph and Diane Bast (Chicago, IL: The Heartland Institute, 1990), pages 297-310.

Chapter Five
Non-Solutions

1. Employee Benefit Research Institute report of March 1992, cited in "State Trends in Uninsured: New Data from EBRI," *Health Benefits Letter #42* (Alexandria, VA: Scandlen Publishing Inc.), page 7.

2. *Statistical Abstract of the U.S.*, 1991, Table 155.

3. Ibid.

4. Cited by John W. Merline, "How Bad is the Uninsured Problem?"

Consumers' Research, August 1990, page 12. See also Katherine Shwartz and Timothy D. McBride, "Spells Without Health Insurance: Distributions of Durations and Their Link to Point-in-Time Estimates of the Uninsured," *Inquiry*, Fall 1990.

5. H.E. Freeman, et al., "Americans Report on Their Access to Health Care," *Health Care Financing Review*, Vol. 11, No. 2, 1989. See also Attiat F. Ott and Wayne B. Gray, *The Massachusetts Health Plan: The Right Prescription?* (Boston, MA: Pioneer Institute for Public Policy Research, 1988), Table 2.15, page 36.

6. J. Needleman, et al., *The Health Care Financing System and the Uninsured* (Washington, DC: Lewin-ICF, April 4, 1991), page viii.

7. Henry J. Aaron, *Serious and Unstable Condition: Financing America's Health Care* (Washington, DC: The Brookings Institution, 1991), page 74.

8. John C. Goodman, "How to Help America's Uninsured," *Consumers' Research*, August 1990, page 13.

9. In 1987, per-capita expenditures for persons under 65 averaged $1,287, whereas spending for persons over 65 averaged $5,306. See Uwe E. Reinhardt, "Health Care Spending and American Competitiveness," *Health Affairs*, Winter 1989, page 11.

10. Employee Benefit Research Institute, *Special Report*, April 1991, page 10.

11. Data from the National Health Interview Survey, as reported in Table 2.11 in Attiat F. Ott and Wayne B. Gray, supra note 5, page 30.

12. Ibid.

13. Employee Benefit Research Institute, supra note 10, page 1.

14. J. Patrick Rooney, "Give Employees Medical IRAs and Watch Costs Fall," *Wall Street Journal*, January 28, 1992.

15. For brief histories of health insurance, see Peter Temin, "An Economic History of American Hospitals," in *Health Care in America*, edited by H.E. Frech III (San Francisco, CA: Pacific Research Institute, 1988), pages 75-102; and Aldona Robbins, Gary Robbins, and Richard Rue, "Mandated and Public Health Insurance: Implications for Wisconsin," *Research Report* (Milwaukee, WI: The Heartland Institute, 1989).

16. Aaron Wildavsky, *Searching for Safety* (New Brunswick, NJ: Transaction Books, 1988).

17. By December 1991, more than two dozen plans had been introduced in Congress. See "Pressure on for health care reform," *Chicago Tribune*, December 15, 1991.

18. General Accounting Office, *Canadian Health Insurance: Lessons for the United States* (Washington, DC: U.S. Government Printing Office, June 1991), page 27.

19. Edward Neuschler, "Canadian Health Care: The Implications of Public

Health Insurance," *Research Bulletin* (Washington, DC: Health Insurance Association of America, June 1990).

20. "Access to Health Care," *Annals of Internal Medicine*, Volume 112, No. 9, May 1, 1990, page 659.

21. For discussions of rent-seeking and the economics of public bureaucracies see James Buchanan and Gordon Tullock, *The Calculus of Consent* (Ann Arbor, MI: University of Michigan Press, 1962); William A. Niskanen, Jr., *Bureaucracy and Representative Government* (Chicago, IL: Aldine-Atherton, 1971); and Dennis C. Mueller, *Public Choice* (Cambridge, England: Cambridge University Press, 1979 (1987)).

22. Robert B. Ekelund, Jr., and David S. Saurman, *Advertising and the Market Process* (San Francisco, CA: Pacific Research Institute for Public Policy, 1988).

23. See Alistair McGuire, Paul Fenn, and Kenneth Mayhew, editors, *Providing Health Care: The Economics of Alternative Systems of Finance and Delivery* (New York, NY: Oxford University Press, 1991) and "Symposium: International comparisons of health care systems," published in *Health Care Financing Review*, Annual Supplement 1989, pages 49-77. Alain C. Enthoven presents the opening remarks; nearly all respondents call for bringing competition into socialized systems.

24. Edward Neuschler, supra note 19, pages 39-40.

25. General Accounting Office, supra note 18, pages 52-61; Philip Jacobs and Warren Hart, "Admission Waiting Times: A National Survey," *Dimensions in Health Service*, Vol. 67, No. 1, February 1990; and "Waiting Their Turns: A Ten-Province Survey" (Vancouver, BC: The Fraser Institute), March 1993.

26. Steven Globerman with Lorna Hoye, "Waiting Your Turn: Hospital Waiting Lists in Canada," *Critical Issues Bulletin* (Vancouver, British Columbia: Fraser Institute, May 1990).

27. Michael Walker, "From Canada: A Different Viewpoint," *Health Management Quarterly*, Volume XI, No. 1, 1989, page 12.

28. Joan Breckenridge, "Grief, Frustration Left in Wake of Man Who Died on Waiting List," *The Globe and Mail*, Ontario, Canada, January 25, 1989.

29. Michael Walker, "Neighborly Advice on Health Care," *Wall Street Journal*, June 8, 1988, page 24. Steven J. Katz, et al., "British Columbia Sends Patients to Seattle for Coronary Artery Surgery," *Journal of the American Medical Association*, Vol. 266, No. 8, August 28, 1991, pages 1106-1111.

30. Rosie DiManno, "Hard Choices Facing Health Care System," *Toronto Star*, January 28, 1989.

31. Edmund F. Haislmaier, "Perception vs. Reality: Taking a Second Look at

Canadian Health Care," *Backgrounder* (Washington, DC: The Heritage Foundation, January 31, 1991), page 14.

32. *Legislative Alert*, National Association of Health Underwriters, October 1992.

33. Data compiled by The Fraser Institute, Vancouver, British Columbia, from information supplied by Statistics Canada ("Public Finance Historical Data 1965/66 - 1991/92") and Health and Welfare Canada.

34. Edward Neuschler, supra note 19, page 64.

35. Aldona Robbins and Gary Robbins, "What a Canadian-Style Health Care System Would Cost U.S. Employers and Employees," *Policy Report* (Dallas, TX: National Center for Policy Analysis, February 1990).

36. Canadian figures supplied by The Fraser Institute; U.S. figures from *Physician Characteristics and Distribution in the United States* (Chicago, IL: Department of Physician Services, Division of Survey and Data Resources, American Medical Association, 1993). These figures actually understate the difference, as the Canadian figures *include* family practice physicians as specialists; family practitioners are excluded from the U.S. figures.

37. Paul M. Ellwood, Alain C. Enthoven, and Lynn Etheredge, "The Jackson Hole Initiatives for a Twenty-First Century American Health Care System," *Health Economics*, Vol. 1: 149-168, 1992.

38. Alain Enthoven and Richard Kronick, "Universal Health Insurance Through Incentives Reform," *Journal of the American Medical Association*, May 15, 1991, Vol. 265, No. 19, page 2533.

39. Paul M. Ellwood, Alain C. Enthoven, and Lynn Etheredge, supra note 37, page 152. See also Alain C. Enthoven, "Market Forces and Health Care Costs," *Journal of the American Medical Association*, November 20, 1991, page 2752.

40. Paul M. Ellwood, Alain C. Enthoven, and Lynn Etheredge, supra note 37, page 158.

41. Ibid., page 160.

42. Alain Enthoven, "Commentary: Measuring the Candidates on Health Care," *New England Journal of Medicine*, Vol. 327, No. 11, 1992, page 809.

43. For a description and further references, see Aldona Robbins, Gary Robbins, and Richard Rue, supra note 15.

44. Alain Enthoven, "Dr. Enthoven on Building a More Just Health Care System Through Incentives Reform," *Managed Medicine*, Vol. 2 No. 3, 1992, pages 7-15.

45. Paul M. Ellwood, Alain C. Enthoven, and Lynn Etheredge, supra note 37, pages 155-157.

46. Ibid., pages 149, 154, 158.

47. Marion Merrell Dow, *Managed Care Digest, PPO Edition*, 1992.

48. *Health Care Benefits Survey 1991, Report 2, Managed Care Plans* (Princeton, NJ: A. Foster Higgins, 1992), pages 2-3.

49. Congressional Budget Office, *CBO Staff Memorandum*, "The Effects of Managed Care on Use and Costs of Health Services," June 1992, page 18.

50. *Health Care Benefits Survey 1991*, supra note 48.

51. Ibid.

52. Congressional Budget Office, supra note 49, page 14.

53. Robert Miller and Harold Luft, "Perspective: Diversity and Transition in Health Insurance Plans," *Health Affairs*, Vol. 10 #4, Winter 1991, pages 37-47.

54. Congressional Budget Office, supra note 49.

55. Robert Pear, "Budget Official Sees No Savings in Clinton's Health-Care Plan," *The New York Times*, February 3, 1993.

56. In 1991, the younger families had an average annual income of $22,477 and average medical expenses of $1,789, versus the older families' $47,852 average annual income and $5,115 average medical expenses. See Roger Feldman and Byron E. Dowd, "Biased Selection—Fairness and Efficiency in Health Insurance Markets," pages 77-78, in *American Health Care Policy: Critical Issues for Reform*, edited by Robert B. Helms (Washington, DC: AEI Press, 1993).

57. Robert B. Helms, editor, *American Health Care Policy: Critical Issues for Reform* (Washington, DC: AEI Press, 1993), pages 29-30.

58. Paul M. Ellwood, Alain C. Enthoven, and Lynn Etheredge, supra note 37, page 153.

59. Alain Enthoven, supra note 42, page 808.

60. See George Stigler, "The Theory of Economic Regulation," *Bell Journal of Economics*, Spring 1971; Richard Posner, "Theories of Economic Regulation," *Bell Journal of Economics*, Autumn 1974; Yale Brozen, *Is Government the Source of Monopoly?* (Washington, DC: Cato Institute, 1980); William A. Niskanan, Jr., *Bureaucracy and Representative Government* (Chicago, IL: Aldine-Atherton, 1971).

61. Mancur Olson, *The Logic of Collective Action* (Cambridge, MA: Harvard University Press, 1975); E.C. Pasour, Jr., "Economists and Public Policy: Chicago Political Economy Versus Conventional Views," *Public Choice*, Vol. 74, 1992, pages 153-167.

62. See George Stigler, supra note 60.

63. Harold Demsetz, "Why Regulate Utilities?" *Journal of Law and Economics*, April 1968.

64. John Semmens and Dianne Kresich, "Deregulation, Privatization, and Air Travel Safety," *Heartland Policy Study #25* (Chicago, IL: The Heartland Institute, 1989).

65. Edwin S. Mills, "Economic Analysis of Urban Land-Use Controls," in *Current Issues in Urban Economics*, edited by Peter Mieskowski and Mahlon Straszheim (Baltimore, MD: The Johns Hopkins University Press, 1979).

66. Alain Enthoven, "Health Care Costs: Why Regulation Fails, Why Competition Works, How to Get There From Here," *National Journal*, May 26, 1979, page 884.

67. William A. Niskanen, "The Costs of Regulation (continued)," *Regulation*, Cato Institute, Spring 1992.

68. Cited in "The papers that ate America," *The Economist*, October 16, 1992.

69. Alfred E. Kahn, *The Economics of Regulation: Principles and Institutions* (Cambridge, MA: The MIT Press, 1989), page xxiii.

70. "The working population and their dependents account for over 70 percent of the total number of uninsured in the U.S." Charles P. Hall, Jr. and John M. Kuder, "Small Business and Health Care: Results of a Survey" (Washington, DC: The NFIB Foundation, April 1990), page 3.

71. Legislation supported by Sen. Edward Kennedy (D-Mass.), for example, would require employers to provide health insurance to their workers or pay a federal tax tentatively set at about 7 percent of payroll.

72. *The New York Times*, May 26, 1991.

73. *The Washington Post*, December 11, 1991.

74. Roy E. Cordato, "Universal Health Care at Any Cost," *IRET Byline*, Institute for Research on the Economics of Taxation, February 20, 1989.

75. "Health Care's Road to Recovery: Address the Cost and Access Problems Now," *Special Report* (Washington, DC: U.S. Chamber of Commerce, September 23, 1991), page 2.

76. John C. Goodman, Gary Robbins, and Aldona Robbins, "Mandating Health Insurance," *Policy Report* (Dallas, TX: National Center for Policy Analysis, February 1989), page 14.

77. Jerry Geisel, "'Pay-or-pay' proposals hit," *Business Insurance*, January 13, 1992, page 1.

78. Ibid., page 37.

79. John C. Goodman, supra note 8.

80. Alain Enthoven, supra note 42.

81. Albert W. Snoke, MD, *Hospitals, Health and People* (New Haven, CT: Yale University Press, 1987), page 109.

82. See, for example, Richard H. Crossman, editor, *The God That Failed* (New York, NY: Bantam Books, 1965 (reprint of 1949 edition)), especially essays by Louis Fischer and Ignazio Silone.

83. See, for example, John Kenneth Galbraith, *Economics & The Public Purpose* (Boston, MA: Houghton Mifflin Company, 1973), page 281.

84. Office of Health Economics (Great Britain), *Compendium of Health Statistics*, 6th edition (London, England: OHB, 1987), Section 3, page 52.

85. Office of Health Economics, *End Stage Renal Failure* (London, England: OHB, 1980), pages 3 and 6.

86. George Onos, "UK Moves Toward Private Health Insurance," Presentation to the Society of Actuaries, Chicago, Illinois, February 17, 1989.

87. Christopher M. Davis, "The Soviet health system: a national health service in a socialist society," in *Success and Crisis in National Health Systems*, edited by Mark G. Field (London: Routledge, 1989), page 244.

88. Ibid.

89. *The New Soviet Society* (final text of the Program of the Communist Party of the Soviet Union), annotations and introduction by Herbert Ritvo (New York, NY: The New Leader, 1962), pages 60-61.

90. Christopher M. Davis, supra note 87, page 252.

91. The newspaper is *Komsomolskaya Pravda*.

92. Charles Wolfe, Jr., *Markets or Governments: Choosing Between Imperfect Alternatives* (Cambridge, MA: The MIT Press); Randall Fitzgerald, *When Government Goes Private: Successful Alternatives to Public Services* (New York, NY: Universe Books, 1988); Gabriel Roth, *The Private Provision of Public Services in Developing Countries* (London: Oxford University Press, 1987); E.S. Savas, *Privatizing the Public Sector* (Chatham, NJ: Chatham House Publishers, Inc., 1982); and Steve H. Hanke, editor, *Prospects for Privatization* (New York, NY: Academy of Political Science, 1987).

93. Myron Lieberman, *Privatization and Educational Choice* (New York, NY: St. Martin's Press, 1989); Joel Spring, *The American School 1642-1985* (New York, NY: Longman, Inc., 1986); James S. Coleman and Thomas Hoffer, *Public and Private High Schools: The Impact of Communities* (New York, NY: Basic Books, Inc., 1987); and Robert B. Everhart, editor, *The Public School Monopoly* (San Francisco, CA: Pacific Institute for Public Policy Research, 1982).

94. John C. Weicher, editor, *Private Innovations in Public Transit* (Washington, DC: American Enterprise Institute for Public Policy Research, 1988); Gabriel Roth and Anthony Shephard, *Wheels Within Cities: Private Alternatives to Public Transport* (London: The Adam Smith Institute, 1984); Ronald F. Kirby, et al., *Para-Transit: Neglected Options for Urban Mobility* (Washington, DC: The Urban Institute); and

Charles A. Lave, editor, *Urban Transit: The Private Challenge to Public Transportation* (San Francisco, CA: Pacific Institute for Public Policy Research, 1985).

95. Douglas K. Adie, *Monopoly Mail: Privatizing the U.S. Postal Service* (New Brunswick, NJ: Transaction Publishers, 1989); Peter J. Ferrara, editor, *Free the Mail: Ending the Postal Monopoly* (Washington, DC: Cato Institute, 1990); and Robert Albon, *Private Correspondence: Competition or Monopoly in Australia's Postal Service* (St. Leonard's, Australia, 1985).

96. Alistair McGuire, Paul Fenn, and Kenneth Mayhew, supra note 23, pages 5-45.

97. For responses from health economists, see Victor R. Fuchs, *Who Shall Live?* (New York, NY: Basic Books, Inc., 1974), pages 18-21; Timothy Besley, "The Demand for Health Care and Health Insurance," in Alistair McGuire, Paul Fenn, and Kenneth Mayhew, supra note 23, pages 46-64; and Henry J. Aaron, supra note 7, page 13.

98. See Laurence S. Seidman, "A Government Health Plan for Free-Marketeers," *Wall Street Journal*, July 22, 1991; and Victor Fuchs, ibid.

Chapter Six
Better Solutions

1. Louise B. Russell, "Medical Care Costs," in *Setting National Priorities: The 1978 Budget*, edited by Joseph A. Pechman (Washington, DC: The Brookings Institution, 1977), pages 205-206.

2. Jesse Hixson, "National Medical Spending: Where Does the Money Go?" (Chicago, IL: American Medical Association Center for Health Policy Research, February 1992), page 8.

3. "A Tax Cap for Health Reform," *The New York Times*, January 22, 1993.

4. John C. Goodman and Gerald L. Musgrave, "Controlling Health Care Costs with Medical Savings Accounts" (Dallas, TX: National Center for Policy Analysis, February 1992).

5. J. Patrick Rooney, "Give Employees Medical IRAs and Watch Costs Fall," *The Wall Street Journal*, January 28, 1992; William Raspberry, "Health Care Giveaway," *The Washington Post*, January 15, 1992.

6. John C. Goodman and Gerald L. Musgrave, supra note 4, page 28.

7. Ibid.

8. Milton Friedman, "The Folly of Buying Health Care at the Company Store," *The Wall Street Journal*, February 3, 1993.

9. NCPA Health Care Task Force, *An Agenda for Solving America's Health Care Crisis* (Dallas, TX: National Center for Policy Analysis, 1990).

Index

Authors

JOSEPH L. BAST is president of The Heartland Institute and author or editor of over a dozen policy studies and three books: *We Can Rescue Our Children: The Cure for Chicago's Public School Crisis* (1988); *Coming Out of the Ice: A Plan to Make the 1990s Illinois' Decade* (1989); and *Rebuilding America's Schools: Vouchers, Tax Credits, and Privatization* (1991).

RICHARD C. RUE is a policy analyst for The Heartland Institute. He is the coauthor of "Mandated and Public Health Insurance: Implications for Wisconsin," a Heartland *Research Report* (1989).

STUART A. WESBURY, JR., PH.D. has been a pharmacist, hospital administrator, university professor, and president and CEO of the American College of Healthcare Executives. He is currently senior vice president of Tribrook Management Consultants, located in Westmont, Illinois.

Publisher

THE HEARTLAND INSTITUTE is a nonprofit research and education organization focusing on state and local public policy issues. Since 1984 its research has been used by concerned citizens across the country to cut taxes and reduce government spending.

Heartland is a genuinely independent source of research and commentary: It is not affiliated with any political party, business, or foundation. It does not accept government funds and does not conduct "contract" research for special interest groups. Its activities are tax-exempt under Section 501(c)(3) of the Internal Revenue Code.

Heartland publications have been called "among the premier economic documents being produced anywhere today." In addition to occasional books, The Heartland Institute publishes *Heartland Policy Studies*, in-depth studies 28 to 40 pages in length; *Heartland Perspectives*, opinion essays three to four pages in length, released twenty times a year; and *Intellectual Ammunition*, a magazine sent to every governor, state legislator, and state constitutional officer in the U.S.

Offices of The Heartland Institute are located in Chicago, Cleveland, Detroit, Kansas City, Milwaukee, and St. Louis. Each office is locally supported and produces publications and educational programs that respond to specific state and local needs.

For further information, call 312/427-3060 or write to The Heartland Institute, 634 South Wabash Avenue, Second Floor, Chicago, Illinois 60605.

■ ■ ■

The Heartland Institute